NATIONAL GEOGRAPHIC

ANGRY BIRDS™
FEATHERED FUN

NATIONAL GEOGRAPHIC

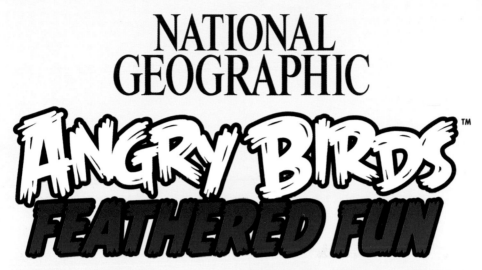

ANGRY BIRDS™
FEATHERED FUN
Facts, Fill-ins, and Fascinating Trivia

FOREWORD BY PETER VESTERBACKA

NATIONAL GEOGRAPHIC

Washington, D.C.

Published by the National Geographic Society, 1145 17th Street N.W., Washington, D.C. 20036

ISBN: 978-1-4262-1389-2

The National Geographic Society is one of the world's largest nonprofit scientific and educational organizations. Its mission is to inspire people to care about the planet. Founded in 1888, the Society is member supported and offers a community for members to get closer to explorers, connect with other members, and help make a difference. The Society reaches more than 450 million people worldwide each month through *National Geographic* and other magazines; National Geographic Channel; television documentaries; music; radio; films; books; DVDs; maps; exhibitions; live events; school publishing programs; interactive media; and merchandise. National Geographic has funded more than 10,000 scientific research, conservation, and exploration projects and supports an education program promoting geographic literacy.

For more information, visit **www.nationalgeographic.com.**
National Geographic Society
1145 17th Street N.W.
Washington, D.C. 20036-4688 U.S.A.

For information about special discounts for bulk purchases, please contact
National Geographic Books Special Sales: **ngspecsales@ngs.org**

For rights or permissions inquiries, please contact National Geographic Books Subsidiary Rights:
ngbookrights@ngs.org

This book was developed and designed in conjunction with Walter Foster Publishing,
a division of Quarto Publishing Group USA Inc.
Printed in China
14/WFP/1

Contents

Foreword: Fancy Yourself as an Egg-spert? **6**

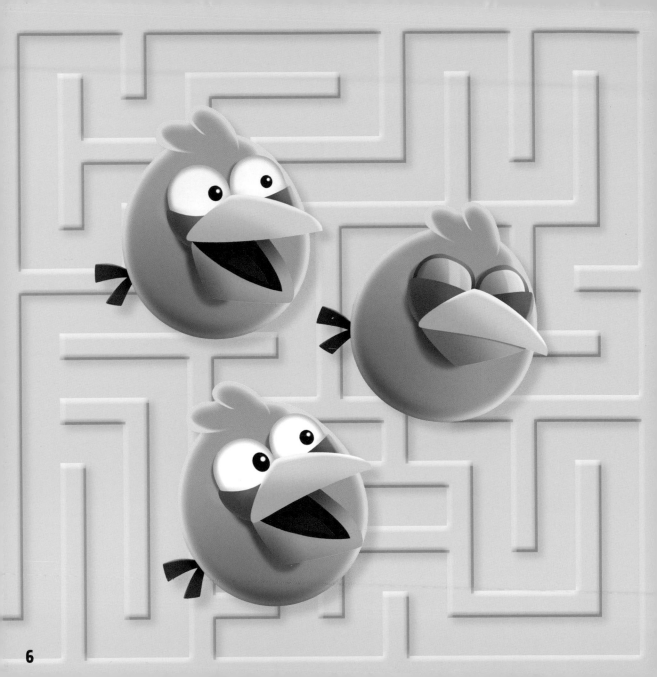

FANCY YOURSELF AS AN EGG-SPERT?

In late 2009, a group of bad-tempered birds took the world by storm when the first Angry Birds game landed on mobile devices. Angry Birds celebrated its 5th "bird-day" in November 2014—compared to the roughly 200,000 years that humans have been around, the 250 million years when dinosaurs ruled the Earth, or the 4.54 billion years Earth has existed, that doesn't seem like such a long time!

They've fitted a lot into a short space of time though. This fun-filled book is packed with brain-teasing activities set in some of the faraway places Angry Birds and National Geographic have traveled together since 2011—the world of the dinosaurs, space, the deepest depths of the rain forest . . . You name it, Red, Chuck and the flock have been there! Discover all their zany findings here, learn about our universe and have some fun along the way.

Last one to Mars is a rotten egg!

Peter Vesterbacka
Mighty Eagle
Rovio Entertainment Ltd.

LEVEL 1 > *AROUND THE WORLD*

Around the world, there are countless reasons to party and explore!

Nicknamed the Bird's Nest, the National Stadium was built for the 2008 Summer Olympics hosted by Beijing, China.

HOME ON EARTH

Each of us has a place we call home. And in our home, we have traditions, like eating dinner as a family or celebrating birthdays with cake and ice cream.

Home is not just the building we live in. It's our community, our city, and even our country. There are homes all around the world. And the people within them have their own neighbors, friends, and families. They even have their own traditions. But we all have something in common: We all call the planet Earth our home!

One of the most fun parts of learning about other places—and even traveling to them—is learning about the people and their special traditions. And no tradition is more fun than a celebration!

So, let's take a flight to some far-off lands and discover where these other homes are located . . . and how the people who live there throw a party!

BIRD'S EYE VIEW

The little planet we call home has a total surface area of 196,900,000 million square miles! That's a lot of zeroes! Because the Earth is so vast, we can't really get a good view of it from on the ground. But when we take to the air, it all comes into focus. We can see our seven continents, wide spans of oceans and seas, and all sorts of amazing geographical places. From tallest mountain to largest lake, you can check out some of the record holders for yourself at right.

LARGEST FRESHWATER LAKE
Lake Superior
31,700 sq mi (82,100 sq km)

NORTH AMERICA

PACIFIC OCEAN

EQUATOR

Amazon River

LONGEST MOUNTAIN RANGE
Andes
4,500 mi (7,200 km)

SOUTH AMERICA

Just show me where it's sunniest!

12

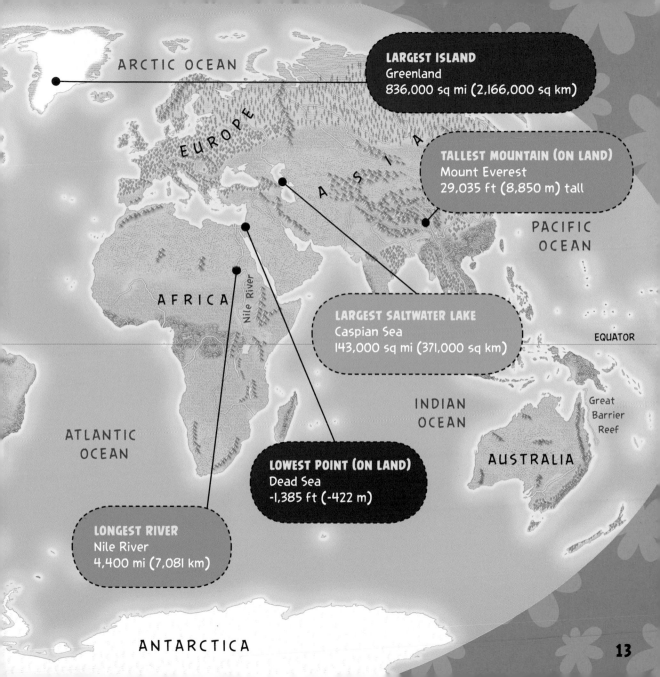

ARCTIC OCEAN

LARGEST ISLAND
Greenland
836,000 sq mi (2,166,000 sq km)

EUROPE

ASIA

TALLEST MOUNTAIN (ON LAND)
Mount Everest
29,035 ft (8,850 m) tall

PACIFIC OCEAN

AFRICA

Nile River

LARGEST SALTWATER LAKE
Caspian Sea
143,000 sq mi (371,000 sq km)

EQUATOR

INDIAN OCEAN

Great Barrier Reef

ATLANTIC OCEAN

AUSTRALIA

LOWEST POINT (ON LAND)
Dead Sea
-1,385 ft (-422 m)

LONGEST RIVER
Nile River
4,400 mi (7,081 km)

ANTARCTICA

13

CONTINENTS

The Earth is mostly water—it makes up about 70% of our planet's surface!
The rest consists of landmasses broken up into seven unique continents.

CONTINENTS AROUND THE WORLD

NAME	SIZE	COUNTRIES	LARGEST COUNTRY	SMALLEST COUNTRY	LARGEST CITY
AFRICA	11,608,000 sq mi (30,065,000 sq km)	54	Algeria	Seychelles	Lagos, Nigeria
ANTARCTICA	5,100,000 sq mi (13,209,000 sq km)				
ASIA	17,208,000 sq mi (44,570,000 sq km)	46	People's Republic of China	Maldives	Tokyo, Japan
AUSTRALIA	2,970,000 sq mi (7,692,000 sq km)	1			Sydney
EUROPE	3,841,000 sq mi (9,947,000 sq km)	46	Russia	Vatican City	London, England
NORTH AMERICA	9,499,000 sq mi (24,474,000 sq km)	23	Canada	St. Kitts and Nevis	Mexico City, Mexico
SOUTH AMERICA	6,880,000 sq mi (17,819,000 sq km)	12	Brazil	Suriname	São Paulo, Brazil

I like this Antarctica place. It's the only continent without pigs!

Q & A: CONTINENTS

1. On what continent will you find the world's longest river?_____

2. What's the largest city in Europe? In Asia?

_____

3. What's the smallest country in South America?

_____

4. What's the world's largest freshwater lake? What continent is it on? _____

5. Are Australia and Antarctica north or south of the Equator? _____

Turn to page 154 for the answers.

CELEBRATIONS

No matter where you live in the world, chances are you've attended a party in your lifetime. After all, we all love to celebrate!

People all around the world mark important events, from birthdays to holidays like New Year's Eve. We sometimes observe these events in different ways—such as the way Jewish families attach importance to thirteenth birthdays, whereas Hispanic families make an event out of the fifteenth. And at times, we even observe different timelines—for example, the Chinese New Year doesn't land on January 1st.

Some traditions are worldwide, others are local or specific to a cultural group. But no matter whether big or small, a party, an event, or a festival, there's one thing all these celebrations have in common: They're about having fun and sharing the joy of the occasion with other people—friends, family, neighbors, and even strangers!

ARE YOU A PARTY BIRD?

Are you the center of the celebration? Or, do you like to let others squawk the loudest during parties? Answer these questions to find out!

When you hear your favorite song, you will be the first on the dance floor:
☐ Yes ☐ No

At a gathering, you will always introduce yourself to people you don't know:
☐ Yes ☐ No

When your friend breaks out the party games, you can't wait to participate:
☐ Yes ☐ No

Your best friend just came down with the flu, no problem, you'll go to the party solo:
☐ Yes ☐ No

On a Saturday afternoon, you would rather round up some friends than quietly watch a movie:
☐ Yes ☐ No

If you answered mostly YES: you're a party bird, all right!

If you answered mostly NO: you have no problem letting others squawk the loudest during parties!

CHINESE NEW YEAR

Chinese New Year is one of the most important Chinese holidays. It is also the most spectacular. The 15-day festival consists of many celebrations, including the traditional New Year's Eve feast. As morning and the new year approach, loud firecrackers are lit to frighten away evil spirits. On Chinese New Year's Day, there are parades and public celebrations, many featuring a dragon dance.

A festive dragon dance welcomes the Chinese New Year in Taiyuan, China.

WHAT YEAR IS IT?

Because it is based on the lunar calendar, Chinese New Year falls on a different day every year, usually in late January or early February in conjunction with the first new moon of the year. In Chinese tradition, each new year is ruled by a different animal. There are twelve animals that make up the Chinese Zodiac, and their different personality traits will influence your life based on the year you were born.

THE CHINESE ZODIAC

ANIMAL	RAT	OX	TIGER	RABBIT	DRAGON	SNAKE	HORSE	SHEEP	MONKEY	ROOSTER	DOG	PIG
BIRTH YEAR	1948	1949	1950	1951	1952	1953	1954	1955	1956	1957	1958	1959
	1960	1961	1962	1963	1964	1965	1966	1967	1968	1969	1970	1971
	1972	1973	1974	1975	1976	1977	1978	1979	1980	1981	1982	1983
	1984	1985	1986	1987	1988	1989	1990	1991	1992	1993	1994	1995
	1996	1997	1998	1999	2000	2001	2002	2003	2004	2005	2006	2007
	2008	2009	2010	2011	2012	2013	2014	2015	2016	2017	2018	2019
	2020	2021	2022	2023	2024	2025	2026	2027	2028	2029	2030	2031

FLY INTO THE NEW YEAR WITH THIS PARTY PUZZLER!

ACROSS

3. Type of dance seen at a Chinese New Year's parade

5. Chinese Zodiac animal if you were born in 1979

7. This type of calendar determines the date of the new year

9. Number of animals in the Chinese Zodiac

DOWN

1. First animal in the Chinese Zodiac

2. Chinese Zodiac animal if you were born in 2005

4. Your Chinese Zodiac animal is based on your _____ year

6. Firecrackers are used to frighten away _____ spirits

8. Traditional Chinese New Year's Eve celebration

Hey, watch out for the Year of the PIG!

Turn to page 154 for the answers.

CARNIVAL

When mysterious masks, fancy costumes, and colorful parades appear in Venice, it's time for Carnival (Carnevale in Italian), a two-week party filled with delicious foods and grand balls. Both a Christian holiday and a cultural phenomenon, Carnival is celebrated every year in the weeks leading up to Lent, the 40-day period that starts on Ash Wednesday and ends on Easter Sunday. During this time, many Roman Catholics historically give up rich foods like meat, milk, and cheese. So during Carnival, people indulge in foods and fun before they go off-limits.

In Venice, competition is more festive than fierce for the best mask.

FOOD, FLOATS, AND FUN

In many cultures, Carnival is a celebration like in Venice—just ask anyone who's attended the famed festivities in Rio de Janeiro! New Orleans has its own take on Carnival called Mardi Gras (French for "Fat Tuesday"), with floats and beads filling the streets. In Canada, the weather turns the celebration into a winter fest. And in some places, it's all about the food: Pancake Day started when a woman was racing to use the last of her "fat" before Lent, but now it's become a fun annual competition!

CARNIVAL CELEBRATIONS AROUND THE WORLD		
NAME	LOCATION	SIGHTS & SOUNDS
CARNEVALE	VENICE, ITALY	GRAND MASKED BALL AND PARADES
CARNIVAL	RIO, BRAZIL	COLORFUL COSTUMES AND SAMBA DANCING
MARDI GRAS	NEW ORLEANS, U.S.A.	PARADE FLOATS AND BEADS
WINTER CARNIVAL	QUEBEC, CANADA	NIGHT PARADES AND SNOW SCULPTURES
PANCAKE DAY	VARIOUS LOCATIONS; ENGLAND	PANCAKE RACES

A festive performer is dressed in a vibrant, extravagant costume at Rio de Janeiro's Carnival celebration, the most famous and largest Carnival celebration in the world.

APRIL FOOLS' DAY

The first of April is one day when practical jokes and pranks reign supreme. The holiday's origins are a bit murky, but many believe that it evolved out of changing traditions surrounding the start of a new calendar year. For many centuries in Europe, the year had traditionally begun in the spring. When the Gregorian calendar was adopted in the 16th century, the beginning of the year was moved back to January. But not everyone observed the shift, and the people who clung to the old ways were teased and called "April fools." As the years passed, a new custom evolved into poking fun at everybody.

On April 1, 1957, many British TV viewers were fooled by the BBC's Swiss spaghetti tree hoax.

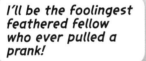

I'll be the foolingest feathered fellow who ever pulled a prank!

JOKING AROUND

Today, most people play small jokes on their friends and family: a whoopee cushion here, a short-sheeted bed there. But larger organizations got in on the fun, too. In 1957, a British TV "documentary" aired, which showed Swiss farmers harvesting spaghetti from trees; many viewers were fooled and called the BBC to see where they could purchase a spaghetti tree!

PULLING THE PERFECT PRANK!

Imagine it's April Fools' Day!
Fill in the blanks to create a story about your practical joke.

April 1st is finally here! It's the day when everyone

plays a _____ on their family and friends!
         NOUN

This year, I am planning the perfect prank—it involves

lots and lots of _____ and _____.
                  PLURAL NOUN   PLURAL NOUN

When _____ gets home from the
          NAME

_____, it will be a _____ surprise!
     PLACE   ADJECTIVE

This is what I will do...

First, I will place a _____ under the cushion
                          NOUN

of the chair. And then, I will hang some _____
                                              ADJECTIVE

_____ from the trees. I might even attempt to
     NOUN

_____ a sign on someone's back! It's all for fun,
     VERB

though. I'm sure everyone will _____
                                      VERB

when they find out it's just a _____!
                                    NOUN

INTI RAYMI

To the sun-worshipping ancient Inca of South America, the winter solstice marked the beginning of a new year and a new solar cycle. On that day, they performed the rite of Inti Raymi, during which they thanked their sun god. The ancient festival lasted nine days and took place in what is known today as Cusco, Peru.

SUN WORSHIPPERS

Today, Inti Raymi lasts a week, and a reenactment of the ancient sun ceremony takes place on June 24, the winter solstice in South America. Locals play different parts in the ritual; one of the most important is the Sapa Inca, or the emperor, who leads much of the ceremony. Other participants dress up as Inca royalty, priests, and other court officials. They gather in front of the Temple of the Sun to hear the Sapa Inca's invocation before the procession moves to the town center, and then finally ascends the Cusco hillsides to the ancient fortress, Sacsahuaman. It's a breathtaking sight that attracts hundreds of thousands of people to Cusco each year.

HOLIDATA

DATE: JUNE 24

LOCATION: CUSCO, PERU

FIRST OBSERVED: CIRCA 13TH CENTURY B.C.

SIGHTS: NATIVE INCA COSTUME

SOUNDS: INVOCATIONS TO THE SUN GOD

Rise and shine!

Authentic Inca outfits make the Inti Raymi celebration a colorful spectacle to behold.

RUNNING OF THE BULLS

One of Spain's most famous events, the Encierro, or running of the bulls, is part of an eight-day festival held in Pamplona in honor of San Fermin, the patron saint of the region. Celebrated every year from July 6 to 14, the fiesta attracts spectators from all over the world who flock to see the brave (or perhaps foolish) people who run with bulls through the streets of the town's old quarter. The Encierro began as a way to get bulls from outside the city to the bullfighting ring inside; the tradition has grown over the years, attracting as many as 6,000 runners a day.

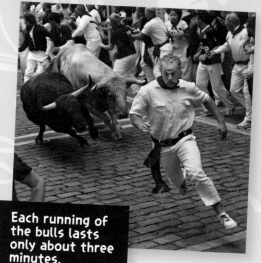

Each running of the bulls lasts only about three minutes.

HOLIDATA

DATE: JULY 6 TO 14

LOCATION: PAMPLONA, SPAIN

FIRST OBSERVED: CIRCA 14TH CENTURY

SIGHTS: PEOPLE RUNNING FROM BULLS

SOUNDS: SNORTING BULLS, BOOMING ROCKETS

ON YOUR MARKS!

Every morning, the runners, who must be over 18, gather and chant three traditional prayers for protection. At eight o'clock, two rockets launch, six bulls charge out of their corral, and the runners take off. The full distance to the ring is roughly 900 yards (825 meters), but most runners do not make it the whole way. They must hop out of the way when the bulls get too close. When the bulls reach the bullring, a third rocket is launched. The fourth rocket lets everyone know that the bulls are safely in the corral and the running of the bulls has ended for the day.

RUNNING OF THE BULLS MAZE

Now it's your turn! Outrun the bull, and find your way to safety.

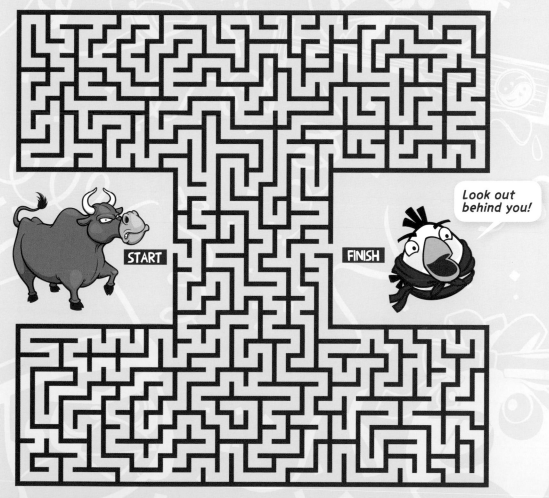

Look out behind you!

START

FINISH

Turn to page 154 for the answers.

THE SUMMER OLYMPICS

Every four years, the Summer Olympics roll around. One lucky city gets to host the games, and spectators come to see the world's top athletes compete for the coveted prize: an Olympic gold medal.

GOING FOR GOLD

The ancient Olympic games were held 3,000 years ago to honor the god Zeus—the first written records date to 776 B.C. when a cook named Coroebus won a footrace called the *stade* (the origin of the word "stadium"). The games fell out of favor during the Roman Empire, and weren't revived until 12 centuries later. The first modern Olympic Games was held in 1896 in Athens, Greece. More than 240 athletes from 14 countries came to compete in 9 different sports, including the marathon, fencing, and wrestling. The games have grown since then: When the Olympics returned to Athens in 2004, nearly 11,000 athletes from a record 201 countries competed for the gold in 28 thrilling summer sports.

Rhythmic gymnastics became an Olympic sport in 1984.

HOLIDATA

DATE: HELD EVERY FOUR YEARS IN AUGUST

LOCATION: WORLDWIDE

FIRST OBSERVED: 1896

SIGHTS: WINNING MEDALS, THRILLING COMPETITION

SOUNDS: NATIONAL ANTHEMS, CHEERING FANS

GO FOR THE GOLD!

Think you're an Olympic contender in Word Search? Quickly find the hidden words below. They appear up, down, forward, backward, and even diagonally!

- [ ] ANCIENT
- [ ] ZEUS
- [ ] STADIUM
- [ ] ATHENS
- [ ] WRESTLING
- [ ] FENCING
- [ ] GOLD
- [ ] SPORTS
- [ ] RACE
- [ ] MEDAL
- [ ] GREECE
- [ ] ATHLETE

```
W S G R E E C E H M V P H P E L W F
R Q O Z J W L L R J V T T A X O I E
E U L D H A L H Z W C O W V R N D N
S B D X H Q Z S X A I F V Q L Y D C
T U S Q P W A S D V Z N C V K N Y I
L S Y I T M I P S A R Y E T B F N N
I K P H O E P R L K A E H E V R M G
N Y V C I D Z N U K C Z T R M N M X
G S H W I K A C Y I E E D S L M E F
A B M N M J N Z X Z L J S F F K M D
I J Y Q M W M I B H D U L A X L X R
S R K V R U Q Y T L H O A I W H D A
T H O F I R G A N C I E N T J X T I
A W X D E V B S C H G P V S L H Q Y
M C A L R M E D A L G N I G F K Z J
W T X W H H S N Q A T H E N S Y M G
S P O R T S U G F P W X I P A C Z Y
```

Turn to page 154 for the answers.

MID-AUTUMN MOON FESTIVAL

As fall grows nearer, the people in China get ready for the Mid-Autumn Moon Festival. On the 15th day of the 8th lunar month (usually in mid- to late September), the moon is big, bright, and appears perfectly round. The holiday has been celebrated for centuries in China, and is one of the most important holidays. Traditions vary by region—for instance, in Hong Kong, dragon dances are popular. Often, people celebrate with their families, gather to appreciate the full moon, and eat tasty mooncakes.

HOLIDATA

DATE: THE 15TH DAY OF THE 8TH CHINESE MONTH (MID- TO LATE SEPTEMBER)

LOCATION: CHINA

EARLY OBSERVANCES: 2,000 YEARS AGO

ALSO KNOWN AS: ZHONG QIU JIE

TRADITIONS: EATING MOON-CAKES, MOON GAZING, FAMILY REUNIONS

MOONCAKES

Eating mooncakes is the most common tradition during the festival across China. Traditionally, mooncakes are round pastries stamped with images of Chang'e, the moon goddess. They are stuffed with different foods that vary by region. Common fillings are red bean paste, sesame paste, lotus seed paste, egg yolks, and sugar. The mooncake's round shape mimics the full moon and symbolizes reunion with family. In the past, people treated this food as a sacrificial offering to the moon, while today it has become a gift to friends and family to wish them good luck and abundance.

A floating dragon lantern lights up the night to celebrate the Mid-Autumn Festival in Beijing, China.

NEW YEAR'S EVE

In many countries around the world, December 31 is the last day of the year. It's time to look back and celebrate the past 12 months, and time to look ahead to the year to come. The earliest known celebration dates back 4,000 years to ancient Babylon. The Romans were the first to place their new year in January in 46 B.C., and Europe began to follow suit in 1582.

HOLIDATA

DATE: DECEMBER 31

LOCATION: GLOBAL

FIRST OBSERVED: 1582

TRADITIONS: EATING LUCKY FOODS, MAKING LOUD NOISES, MAKING RESOLUTIONS

GREETINGS: "HAPPY NEW YEAR!"

A LUCKY HOLIDAY

New Year's Eve traditions bring in the new year with merriment and a little superstition. Many people go to parties, eat lucky foods, make lots of noise, and make resolutions for the coming year. In Spanish-speaking countries, eating 12 grapes, one for each month, will bring good luck. One Latin American tradition says that wearing yellow underwear on New Year's Eve ushers in prosperity. Pigs mean prosperity in Italian, Cuban, Austrian, and Portuguese culture, so pork is on many New Year's Eve menus. Getting together with friends is also a popular tradition: In the U.S., people gather outside in the cold in New York City to watch a giant, glittering ball drop at midnight in Times Square. Nothing like a celebration with shivering folks to warm you up and welcome the new year!

Booming fireworks bring in the New Year over the boats in Sydney Harbor, Australia.

LEVEL 2 DINOSAURS

It's past the time we explore prehistory, when dinosaurs walked the Earth.

UNCOVER CLUES TO THE PAST

Have you ever seen a dinosaur in person? Of course not! That's because they lived in prehistoric times—millions and millions of years ago.

Scientists who study prehistory, called paleontologists, are like detectives. They search for clues in the form of fossils. Dinos didn't draw or write, but they did leave footprints and bones. These survived because they were packed down into mud or sand and preserved. Over time, minerals replaced the original material and turned it into rock. When we look at dinosaur bones, we're viewing fossils—stone replicas.

Fossils can tell us how big the dinosaurs were. Scientific theory tells us the rest. Scientists see the evidence and form hypotheses, or educated guesses, about their meaning. Sometimes they are proven wrong. When they aren't, they become theory.

Are you ready to dig into the past to discover more about dinosaurs?

Lourinhanosaurus

37

PREHISTORY

By definition, "prehistory" is the period of human existence before any written records or recorded history. It also can refer to the time before humans and the invention of writing. It's hard to imagine a time before humans were part of the world! But in reality, humans have only walked the Earth for about 200,000 years. That's just a tiny hiccup in time—the Earth has existed for around 4.5 billion years!

Dinosaurs walked the Earth for 150 million years. That's nearly 1,000 times as long as human beings! Prehistory covers a lot more territory than just the time of the dinosaurs. But when dinosaurs ruled, the Earth was a very interesting place! Let's take a closer look at what life was like in that era.

Archaeopteryx

The first bird flew in the Jurassic period.

38

PREHISTORIC ESCAPE

Explore the past, but don't get lost—quickly find your way back to safety in the present!

START

FINISH

Turn to page 155 for the answer.

AGE OF THE DINOSAURS

Dinosaurs dominated the planet in a time called the Mesozoic Era. But not all the dinosaurs lived at the same time. Just as Neanderthal man doesn't co-exist with modern humans, earlier dinosaurs died off, making room for later generations. Historians break up the Mesozoic Era into distinct time periods, including the Triassic, Jurassic, and Cretaceous. Each period ended when a great tragedy occurred, killing off many species and giving way to new life as a result.

MESOZOIC PERIOD	YEARS AGO	KNOWN FOR
Triassic	250 million to 200 million	The Earth was scorching hot and there wasn't much oxygen to breathe when the first dinosaurs appeared
Jurassic	200 million to 145 million	Dinosaurs started out small but now grew much larger and stranger—some even took flight, dominating the skies
Early Cretaceous	145 million to 100 million	The continents were shifting, separating dinosaur species, and creating many new varieties as they adapted to changes
Late Cretaceous	100 million to 65 million	Dinosaurs had no competition—on land, in air, or under water—but their rule still came to a shocking end

The first flying dinosaurs were feathered and the size of a chicken, but they eventually gave way to *Pteranodon* (seen here) and other large pterosaurs.

TRIASSIC

The beginning of the Triassic period was rather bleak. Scientist aren't exactly sure, but they believe this desolate time was due to volcanic eruptions, climate change, or even a comet that crashed to the Earth. What they do know is that it triggered the extinction of more than 90 percent of the Earth's species!

But some animals did survive and quickly diversified and evolved. The ocean was soon filled with giant reptiles, squid, and the first appearance of coral. The ocean spilled onto the Triassic coast, home of many species of frogs, crocodiles, and turtles. More inland, the first grasshoppers emerged along with spiders, scorpions, and centipedes. And then, in the late Triassic period, the biggest change occurred with the evolution of dinosaurs and the first mammals.

Riojasaurus

Triassic forests were alien places dominated by odd plants and unfamiliar animals, such as the tusked, beaked dicynodont, seen at right.

WHAT'S FOR DINNER?

One way to classify dinosaurs is to divide them into two categories: plant-eaters and meat-eaters.

Plant-eaters, known as herbivores, eat grass, twigs, tree bark, and plants. If you were to look inside a herbivore dinosaur's mouth, you'd discover wide, flat teeth—perfect for grinding foliage. Small-bodied dinosaurs of the bird-hipped variety (called "ornithischian") are an example of Triassic herbivores. But a plant diet didn't prevent other dinosaurs from growing very large!

Meat-eaters, known as carnivores, eat diets consisting mostly of animal flesh and meat. You wouldn't want to look into this mouth, because a carnivore is a hunter with a whole lot of razor-sharp teeth made for tearing things apart. Dinosaurs of the Theropod group are one example of Triassic carnivores. *Tyrannosaurus Rex* hadn't arrived yet in the Triassic, but it's a very famous carnivore.

Lessemsaurus—an herbivorous dinosaur

44

WHICH DINOSAUR ARE YOU?

Dinosaurs are put into two main groups,
carnivores and herbivores! Which one are you?

1. At a friend's barbecue, this will
   be piled high on your plate:
   a. Hot dogs and hamburgers
   b. Potato salad and watermelon slices

2. It's your birthday, and your mom
   offers to make your favorite meal!
   You choose:
   a. Grilled chicken sandwich
   b. Grilled veggie wrap

3. You're headed to the beach and pack
   some snacks. What do you bring?
   a. Beef jerky
   b. Carrot sticks and hummus

4. Your friend is coming over for
   lunch, you'll make:
   a. Chicken nuggets
   b. Fruit and nut salad

YOU ANSWERED MOSTLY A'S:
You're a carnivore! These
hunters ate a lot of meat
(other dinosaurs!).

YOU ANSWERED MOSTLY B'S:
You're an herbivore! These
plant-lovers grazed on leaves,
branches, and grass.

JURASSIC

The Jurassic period was known for its hot, humid, steam-bath-like climate. This was an environmental paradise for palm trees and ferns—even the dry deserts took on a green hue. The oceans and seas were crowded with fish-like dinosaurs, sharks, sponges, and snails. Microscopic plankton scattered through the ocean, turning it red.

On land, dinosaurs were growing to giant sizes. *Brachiosaurus* stretched to 85 feet long! The hunter *Allosaurus* tracked down its prey by walking on two powerful hind legs. *Stegosaurus* was also quite large, and able to protect itself with heavy armor-like skin. Reptiles also took to the skies during the Jurassic period in abundance, along with flying and leaf-hopping insects.

Apatosaurus

Allosaurus (lower right) not only had powerful legs—get a load of those teeth! And its lower jaw could bend outward, making room for bigger bites of meat.

UNDER THE SEA

The warm and stable climate of the Jurassic period resulted in many newly developed types of animals and plants. During this time, the number of different species greatly increased and diversified—especially in the sea.

The waters were plentiful with new invertebrate species like snails, mollusks, and gastropods. Corals grew reefs in the warm water while sharks and rays swam around them. But they were no match for the mega-predators of the deep.

The largest marine hunter was *Plesiosaurus*. Their broad bodies, long necks, and four flippers helped them swiftly zoom through the water after prey. The more fish-shaped reptile, *Ichthyosaurus*, was also a very common carnivore. Paleontologists have discovered smaller fossils inside of larger ones. This leads them to believe *Ichthyosaurus* gave birth to live young instead of eggs! Both were fierce hunters. The previous marine life of the Triassic period remained fixed on the sea floor and could simply not compete with these new fast-moving predators!

Squidlike belemnites were a common food for toothy marine reptiles like icthyosaurs.

48

DINO DROPPING TREATS

A large dino may have dumped up to 4 gallons of stinky stuff at once!
But this recipe is smaller, sweeter, and better smelling.
Have an adult help you bake up a batch.

WHAT YOU WILL NEED

- 2 cups sugar
- 1/4 cup butter
- 4 tablespoons cocoa
- 1/2 cup milk

- 2 cups oats
- 1/2 cup peanut butter
- 1 tablespoon vanilla

WHAT TO DO

1. Mix together the sugar, butter, cocoa, and milk.

2. Heat over medium heat until boiling.

3. Remove from heat.

4. Stir in oats, peanut butter, and vanilla.

5. Scoop up a medium-size ball and drop onto wax paper to cool off and dry.

6. Dig in and enjoy!

Better than bugs!

EARLY CRETACEOUS

During the beginning of the Cretaceous period, dinosaurs ruled the Earth! In fact, new types of dinosaurs emerged. Herd-dwelling dinosaurs migrated to everywhere across the globe, except for frigid Antarctica. Other creatures like frogs, salamanders, crocodiles, and snakes inhabited the coasts. And, shrew-like mammals scampered around in the forest.

But it was the flowering plants that truly flourished during this time. With the help of bees, wasps, ants, and beetles, flowers bloomed big and bold. Magnolia, ficus, and sassafras trees soon outnumbered the previously dominant ferns and conifer plants. Some of these trees and plants even exist today!

Water lilies, such as these blooming in Botswana's Okavango Delta, have a lineage that dates back to the Cretaceous.

All life did well in the Cretaceous, from flowers to sea life and land animals!

LEVEL 2 DINOSAURS

Answer these questions,
and show off how smart you are!

1. Bees, ants, wasps, and beetles help these bloom big and bold:

   _____

2. Herd-dwelling dinosaurs migrated to all of the continents

   except for this, the coldest:

   _____

3. These tree species soon outnumbered the ferns and

   conifers: _____

4. These amphibians lived on the coast during this time:

   _____

5. This slithering reptile was also a coastal inhabitant during

   the Cretaceous period: _____

Turn to page 155 for the answers.

Spinosaurus (meaning "spined lizard") was a meat-eater extraordinaire. His crocodile-like snout made fishing a snap. And with a threatening height of 45 feet and razor-sharp claws, small dinos on land weren't safe from this predator, either.

EVERYTHING EVOLVES

Plants and flowers thrived in the Early Cretaceous period! This helped many dinosaurs, mostly herbivores, multiply during this time. But some did not. *Stegosaurus* was an herbivore with a toothless beak in the front of its mouth. This didn't really allow it to chew its food properly, so to compensate, *Stegosaurus* swallowed stones. These stones in *Stegosaurus*'s stomach helped break down the food its beak could not!

For unknown reasons, *Stegosaurus* was replaced with *Ankylosaurus*. This armored dinosaur walked on four legs and possessed a massive bony club tail. Unlike its ancestor, *Ankylosaurus* had leaf-shaped teeth that were ideal for eating vegetation!

A descendant of *Stegosaurus*, *Ankylosaurus* inherited its ancestor's thick, well-armored skin, along with a tail to thrash around. Instead of stegosaur tail spikes, this dinosaur could swing a tail equipped with a heavy club of skin-covered bones!

Stegosaurus

LATE CRETACEOUS PERIOD

During the beginning of this great period, the continents were forged together in one singular landmass. However, 80 million years later, oceans filled the space between land, and the Earth looked much like it does today. But that's where any similarities end. According to scientists, a giant crater burned into what is now known as the Yucatán Peninsula located in modern-day Mexico. What caused the crater is an unsolved mystery.

Much of the life that evolved over the years—dinosaurs, plants, sea animals—perished during this time. These animals, such as velociraptors, became extinct toward the end of the Cretaceous period, some 65 million years ago. The land, sea, and skies would never be the same.

Velociraptor had feathers like a bird.

We need a crater for pigs!

CRETACEOUS PERIOD CROSSWORD

ACROSS

2. What burned into the Yucatán Peninsula?
3. In which country is the Yucatán Peninsula?
6. How many million years ago did the Cretaceous period end?
7. During the beginning of the Cretaceous period, the continents were one singular _____.

DOWN

1. Along with Jurassic and Cretaceous, which other period was part of the Mesozoic Era?
3. The catastrophic event that changed the Earth forever is a _____.
4. Animals became this during the end of this period
5. It was the end for these great prehistoric creatures

Turn to page 155 for the answers.

NOTHING LASTS FOREVER

This period marks the extinction of dinosaurs. The great herbivores and carnivores of the land perished. And so did the giant predators of the sea. The base of the food chain, plankton, drastically declined. And so did the animals that relied on it for food. Vegetation also withered, and more than half the world's species were eliminated.

A miles-wide asteroid struck Cretaceous Central America

What caused the mass extinction? Scientists have two possible explanations. The first is an asteroid or comet that crashed into the Earth. The second is massive volcanic explosions. Both of these situations would have filled the skies with debris and blocked out the sun's energy. Plants could not survive and destruction would filter down the food chain.

But some species did survive. Most mammals, turtles, crocodiles, salamanders, and frogs escaped the devastation. Birds still soared the skies. And snails, bivalves, starfish, and sea urchins remained intact. We recognize most of these creatures still inhabiting the Earth today.

IT'S ALL RELATIVE

Think you know everything about the dinosaurs now?
The Angry Birds have one more secret to share.

THE TRUTH ABOUT DINO EXTINCTION

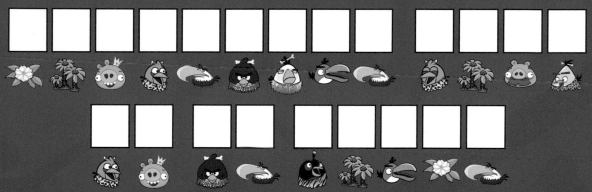

A		E		N		S	
B		I		O		U	
D		L		R		V	

Turn to page 155 for the answers.

59

TIME MARCHES ON

The Mesozoic Era was also called "the age of reptiles," as those were the dominating animals of the land, sea, and sky. Paleontologists have discovered fossils of dinosaurs living during the three major sub-eras: the Triassic, Jurassic, and Cretaceous periods.

Each of these periods also experienced distinct tectonic plate shifts, climate differences, and evolutionary growth. The climate of the Mesozoic varied from very warm to cool periods. Tectonic plates drastically moved and shifted. And animals evolved to new species, thrived, and then sometimes died off.

But what may be considered most fascinating is that this era begins and ends with large mass extinctions, providing space for humans. Some of our questions will remain unanswered. One day, will someone wonder about us?

End of the dinosaurs

This is as close as I get.

Petite *Parksosaurus* attempt to escape wildfires that scientists hypothesize were sparked by the aftermath of an asteroid impact. The extinction of dinosaurs gave way for humans to evolve on earth.

LEVEL 3 SPACE

Let's blast off to space, exploring planets, galaxies, and stars.

WORLDS ABOVE US

Have you ever walked outside on a clear, moonless night and gazed at the thousands of stars sparkling in the sky? From Earth, the stars look like mere twinkling dots—hardly interstellar balls of gas, nearly 13 billion years old! Stars are only one of space's many fascinating elements that continue to intrigue not only scientists and explorers, but also storytellers and musicians.

Through space programs, we have made amazing discoveries about the universe. We now know so much about our moon, the Milky Way, space travel, and our planet. But, there is loads more to learn! In fact, scientists now use a special telescope—the Allen Telescope Array—to listen for signals of intelligent extraterrestrial life. Imagine if your distant cousin was really an alien!

So, let your imagination fly wild! There are great things to discover.

THE SOLAR SYSTEM

It's the sun's gravity that holds the entire solar system together. This array of celestial objects ranges from planets down to asteroids and even dust, stretching from the sun's surface to the distant Oort cloud. The Oort cloud is home to billions of massive ice balls, which if dislodged, fall toward the sun, becoming long-tailed comets. The planets are spread across an enormous distance. In order, they are Mercury, Venus, Earth, Mars, Jupiter, Saturn, Uranus, and Neptune. The closest, Mercury, averages 36 million miles (58 million km) from the sun, and the farthest, Neptune, averages about 2.8 billion miles (4.5 billion km) from the sun. Now that's far out!

The solar system

OUT OF THIS WORLD WORD SEARCH!

Circle each word hidden below.
Words will appear up, down, forward, backward, and diagonally.

- MILKY WAY
- ASTEROID
- ORBITS
- COMET
- PLANET
- SATELLITES
- COSMOS
- SUPERNOVA
- ROCKET
- MOON

```
B  I  C  A  C  D  W  O  S  U  P  E  R  N  O  V  A  I  S
A  H  F  N  N  O  L  S  B  C  M  X  L  L  Y  W  G  T  G
G  J  L  E  A  Y  M  L  Y  O  D  P  K  D  F  E  I  E  C
Y  X  G  G  Q  Y  K  E  B  D  U  V  Y  K  G  B  T  K  M
P  R  Z  X  X  V  I  J  T  Z  R  V  Y  J  R  E  A  J  O
T  E  S  X  W  M  O  J  Y  A  W  J  P  O  N  D  A  B  O
N  Z  K  Q  K  I  C  F  F  Q  W  U  O  A  Z  G  P  Y  N
O  G  W  J  B  L  B  Y  S  A  T  E  L  L  I  T  E  S  E
D  D  H  O  K  K  L  L  D  H  N  P  J  R  K  S  C  Y  S
L  X  Z  O  B  Y  H  N  U  U  H  N  Y  P  M  B  W  E  C
R  G  C  V  W  R  N  S  E  H  L  M  V  G  R  L  J  L
T  M  A  A  M  C  O  S  M  O  S  T  J  F  V  T  G
W  Q  Z  Y  A  F  D  H  H  A  S  T  E  R  O  I  D
A  G  Y  A  K  G  Y  J  L  E  N  C  R  O  S  Z  J
R  O  C  K  E  T  L  X  S  U  D  O  F  B  M  A  I  D
```

Turn to page 156 for the answers.

THE SUN

The sun, the closest star to the Earth and center of our solar system, was born about 4.6 billion years ago. The star is actually a burning ball of ionized gases, composed mainly of hydrogen and helium, with trace amounts of oxygen, carbon, iron, and sulfur. Though it's only average-sized for a star, the sun makes up 99.8% of the entire solar system's mass! At its center, unfathomable heat and pressure cause nuclear fusion to convert half a billion tons of hydrogen into helium every second. If you think it can get hot where you live, imagine this: the core of the sun can reach up to 27,000,000°F (15,000,000°C). That's enough to make the sun's surface temperature, 10,000°F (5,500°C) seem cool!

ASTROFACT

NUCLEAR FUSION IN THE SUN'S CORE GENERATES ABOUT 400 TRILLION TRILLION WATTS OF ENERGY PER SECOND.

SPACE DATA

DISTANCE FROM EARTH: 93 MILLION MILES (150 MILLION KM)

THE SUN HAS ENOUGH ENERGY TO BURN FOR 100 BILLION MORE YEARS, BUT MOST OF THAT TIME IT WOULD BE A COOLING, WHITE DWARF.

The sun as seen by a solar observatory

ROTATION PERIOD:
25.38 EARTH DAYS

SURFACE TEMPERATURE:
9939°F (5504°C)

DIAMETER:
864,000 MILES (1.39 MILLION KM)

MAJOR PLANETS:
8

69

MERCURY

Just slightly larger than Earth's moon—and the smallest major planet in our solar system—Mercury is the closet planet to the sun. It also orbits the sun faster than any other planet. In fact, if you lived on Mercury, one year would last just 88 Earth days!

We've discovered much about Mercury's composition by studying the data collected by NASA'S MESSENGER—the first spacecraft to orbit the planet. Through it, we know that the surface is covered in craters—evidence of former violent collisions.

A false-color image of Caloris Basin, Mercury's largest crater

ASTROFACT

291 OF MERCURY'S CRATERS HAVE OFFICIAL NAMES!

VENUS

Every 19 months, Venus, which is 162 million miles from Earth at its farthest, makes its closest approach to Earth—passing at a mere 24 million miles away! It's hard to believe that this is Earth's closest neighbor. And from simple observation, Venus is similar to our home planet, being almost the same size and structure. But, that's about all they have in common.

Venus's atmosphere is made of carbon dioxide gas and sulfuric acid clouds that trap the sun's heat. This causes temperatures to rise to scorching highs of 860 degrees. Now that's hot! And it never cools off. Even after dark, midnight is just as hot as noon.

Venus

Volcanoes (below) Sif Mons (left) and
Gula Mons (right), Venus

ASTROFACT

PEOPLE REPORT THE
MOST UFO SIGHTINGS
WHEN VENUS IS
CLOSEST TO EARTH.

EARTH

Our planet is a truly amazing place and very unique in our solar system. To begin, nearly 70 percent of the Earth's surface is covered by a liquid-water ocean. It's why Earth is called the "blue planet." This is extraordinary because Earth is the only planet where water can exist as a liquid (rain), solid (ice), and gas (clouds).

The Earth's atmosphere—mostly nitrogen and oxygen—protects us from harmful radiation. Meteors and other destructive objects are also prevented from crashing into the Earth due to the atmosphere. The magnetic surface deflects particles from the solar wind. These protective conditions, plus the distance from the sun, make Earth the only planet known to harbor life.

An artist's rendering shows the Earth, moon, and sun in alignment.

SPACE DATA

DISTANCE FROM THE SUN: 93 MILLION MILES (150 MILLION KM)

ROTATION PERIOD: 24 HOURS

ONE YEAR: 365 DAYS

MOONS: 1

MEMORY GAME

A sharp memory is required to be a successful space scientist! See if you have what it takes by studying this image for sixty seconds, then turn the page to see how many questions you can answer about it.

THE MOON

The Earth and the moon have a unique relationship. Have you ever wondered why there's a "dark side" of the moon? It's an astronomical coincidence. The moon spins on its axis, just like Earth, but the moon's rate of rotation matches the rate of its progression around Earth—it takes about 27.3 Earth days to complete both. Therefore, only one side of the moon is visible toward the Earth, while the other side always faces away. The surface of the moon has been compared to Swiss cheese. That pocked appearance is actually an assemblage of craters caused by celestial objects crashing into the moon's surface. Ouch!

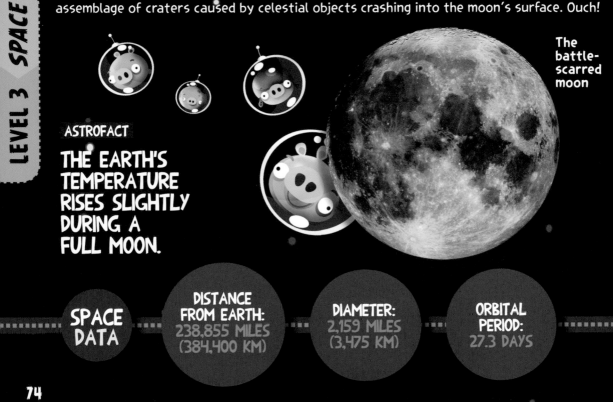

The battle-scarred moon

ASTROFACT

THE EARTH'S TEMPERATURE RISES SLIGHTLY DURING A FULL MOON.

SPACE DATA

DISTANCE FROM EARTH:
238,855 MILES
(384,400 KM)

DIAMETER:
2,159 MILES
(3,475 KM)

ORBITAL PERIOD:
27.3 DAYS

MEMORY QUESTIONS

1. There are two stripes on the pants of the astronaut's space suit. What color are they? _____

2. What country's flag is on the astronaut's shoulder?

   _____

3. With one hand, the astronaut is grasping the space station. What is he doing with his other hand?_____

4. What part of Earth is the astronaut floating over?

   _____

5. How many Angry Birds appear in the image?

   _____

6. What type of "shoes" is the astronaut wearing?

   _____

7. What can be seen on the face mask of the astronaut's helmet?

   _____

Turn to page 156 for the answers.

MARS

Of all the planets, Mars is the most similar to our own. It rotates on its axis every 24.6 hours, creating a day much like ours. It has similar seasons. Mars has its own atmosphere, clouds, and polar caps. One major difference, however, is that Mars is much smaller than Earth. Still, we know Mars well. There have been more than a dozen flybys, orbiters, landers, and rovers, as well as many telescopes here on Earth, that have scanned the Martian surface.

Life on Mars?

We've all seen the old movies about Martians—little green men roaming the red planet—and it's true Mars holds a special place in the human imagination. While we know that these classic aliens might not be there, something else might. Ground-based observers detected methane on Mars, significant because, on its own, the gas should decay within a couple of centuries. Scientists reason that there must be an active source on the planet to replenish the gas, which could mean one of two things: Either an active geothermal process is generating methane and venting it at the surface, or—is there life on Mars?—some sort of biological activity is occurring beneath the surface.

ASTROFACT

IN 1906, AMERICAN ASTRONOMER PERCIVAL LOWELL THEORIZED THAT AN ANCIENT CIVILIZATION BUILT CANALS ON MARS BEFORE DYING OUT.

SPACE DATA

DISTANCE FROM THE SUN: 141.6 MILLION MILES (227.9 MILLION KM)

MARS HAS TWO SMALL MOONS— PHOBOS AND DEIMOS—WHOSE NAMES MEAN "FEAR" AND "PANIC."

The planet Mars

ROTATION PERIOD: 24.6 HOURS

ONE YEAR: 686.9 EARTH DAYS

DIAMETER: 4,222 MILES (6,794 KM)

MOONS: 2

JUPITER

Jupiter is the largest planet in the solar system. So big, in fact, that 1,400 Earths could fit inside of it! But, what's really astonishing is its atmosphere. Jupiter is a speedily spinning planet—one day lasts only 10 Earth hours. Because of this quick rotation, Jupiter's surface looks like a lava lamp. The swirling wind creates bands of color in the thick mix of gases.

There are also spectacular storm systems on Jupiter. The Great Red Spot is the most famous stormy area—and its largest at about twice the size of Earth. It is incredibly persistent, too—this storm has lasted for hundreds of years!

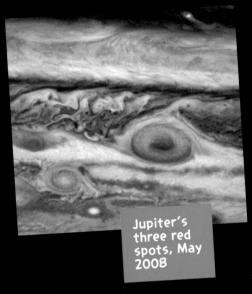

Jupiter's three red spots, May 2008

ASTROFACT

JUPITER'S COLORFUL RUST-COLORED STRIPES ARE MADE OF AMMONIA HYDROSULFIDE—WHICH SMELLS LIKE ROTTEN EGGS.

MEGA MAZE

Navigate your way around the planet Jupiter.

START

FINISH

Turn to page 156 for the answer.

SATURN

The ringed planet is probably the most recognizable of all the planets. It's definitely the most distant planet you can see with the naked eye. Although it is the second largest planet, its density is less than that of water. This means, if Saturn were to be placed in a body of water, it would float!

Saturn's rings are made up of billions of icy particles, some small like a grain of sand and others as big as boulders. The outermost rings are eight million miles from the planet! But, Saturn's rings may not last forever—scientists believe that the rings will eventually disappear.

ASTROFACT

ONE TRIP AROUND THE SUN TAKES SATURN MORE THAN 29 EARTH YEARS, BUT ONE DAY ON SATURN LASTS JUST UNDER 11 HOURS.

SPACE DATA

DISTANCE FROM THE SUN: 885.9 MILLION MILES (1.4 BILLION KM)

ANCIENT MESOPOTAMIAN ASTRONOMERS CALLED SLOW-MOVING SATURN "THE OLD SHEEP."

I prefer "The Old Piggy."

A Cassini spacecraft image of Saturn. Cassini has been exploring Saturn for over 10 years!

ROTATION PERIOD: 10.8 HOURS

ONE YEAR: 29.5 EARTH YEARS

DIAMETER: 74,898 MILES (120,536 KM)

MOONS: 62 (53 NAMED)

URANUS

One of the coldest major planets, Uranus is made largely of water and frozen methane—making it appear turquoise. It is considered an ice giant. In fact, the winter season lasts 21 Earth years on this chilly planet!

Uranus is special for another reason, too: it spins on its side. Scientists often ponder what knocked Uranus sideways. The most common answer is that it collided with another planet.

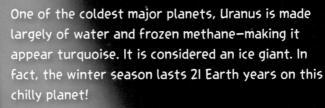

Enhanced color image of Uranus

ASTROFACT

WINDS ON URANUS HAVE BEEN CLOCKED AT 360 MILES AN HOUR (579 KM/H).

Uranus (blue-green in background) and its five largest moons

NEPTUNE

If you were standing on Neptune, the sun would appear as a dazzling bright star in a black sky. It's the most distant major planet in our solar system. Although it is an ice giant like Uranus, Neptune has intense turbulent weather.

This planet's fierce storms with supersonic winds can be nine times more powerful than hurricane winds on Earth—more than 1,200 miles an hour!

Neptune

ASTROFACT

NEPTUNE'S MOON TRITON MAY BE A KIDNAPPED KUIPER BELT OBJECT, CAPTURED BY THE PLANET'S GRAVITY MILLIONS OF YEARS AGO.

Does it need rescuing?

PLANETS QUIZ

1. Number of Mercury's craters that have official names:

_____

2. Venus's atmosphere is made of _____ _____
gas and _____ _____ clouds.

3. Earth is the only planet where water can exist in its three
different states: _____, _____, and
_____.

4. Mars's two small moons, _____ and _____,
mean "fear" and "panic."

5. The largest planet in the solar system, Jupiter could fit this
many Earths inside it: _____.

6. Saturn's outermost rings are this many miles from the planet:

_____.

7. How fast can the winds on Uranus blow? _____

8. Neptune's moon _____ may be a kidnapped
Kuiper Belt object.

Turn to page 156 for the answers.

PLUTO

After enjoying seventy-six years in the big leagues, Pluto was demoted from the planetary ranks in 2006. Pluto was the smallest planet with a diameter of just 1,430 miles (2,301 km), and the farthest from the sun. But because it fails to clear its orbit of debris, it is now classified as a "plutoid," a new class of solar system objects. Pluto and other transneptunian objects inhabit the Kuiper belt, a giant, scattered disk beyond Neptune, containing perhaps a million rocky and icy "leftovers" from the formation of the solar system.

ASTROFACT

AN 11-YEAR-OLD GIRL, VENETIA BURNEY, NAMED PLUTO.

Looking back at the sun from Pluto's surface

SPACE DATA

DISTANCE FROM THE SUN: 3.7 BILLION MILES (5.9 BILLION KM)

ROTATION PERIOD: -6.4 HOURS (RETROGRADE)

ONE YEAR: 247.9 EARTH YEARS

COMETS

During the solar system's formation, billions of clusters of frozen gas and dust also formed and were swept away to the farthest distances. Most stay put, but if any are nudged into a new orbit closer to the sun, they become comets. The glowing head, or coma, of a comet is formed around the frozen nucleus as comets warm up approaching the sun and release stored gases. A flow of charged ions is shaped by the solar wind as a magnificent gas tail. At the same time, a stream of dust forms a second tail. One of the most famous, Halley's comet, has had appearances dating back as far as the second century B.C.

ASTROFACT

A COMET'S NUCLEUS IS MADE OF DIRTY ICE ABOUT AS DARK AS FRESH TAR.

Comet McNaught above the Andes Mountains, January 2007

SPACE DATA	NAME: COMET HALLEY	SIZE: 5 X 9.3 MILES (8X15 KM)	ONE YEAR: 76 EARTH YEARS	NEXT RETURN: 2061

STARS

The earliest stars formed nearly 13.5 billion years ago. Some stars faded away—these are called white dwarfs—and others exploded as supernovae.

Our sun, an average size star, is neither the biggest nor the smallest. The smallest stars are called red drawfs and can burn up to ten trillion years. Supergiants, the largest stars, are 1,000 times bigger than the sun! The biggest, called Betelgeuse, is in the Orion constellation. It may be at the end of its star-life and could explode as a supernova in the next few thousand to a million years.

ASTROFACT

RED DWARFS ARE THE MOST COMMON STARS IN THE UNIVERSE.

But are they the angriest?

ASTROFACT

THE HOTTEST STARS SHINE BLUE.

STARRY, STARRY NIGHT STAR MAP

Use a dark marker to connect the dots and discover this famous constellation.
Take it outside and see if you can find it in the night sky.

3

2

5

1

4

6

7

Turn to page 157 for the answers.

STARGAZING

Sky watching was one of the earliest forms of entertainment—way before movies and video games held our attention. It's a hobby that's still popular today, appealing to city dwellers and country inhabitants alike.

Beginning this activity requires "gear" as simple as your two eyes. Remember: venturing outside is always the first step! See the next page for some stargazing tips!

A cluster of young, hot stars in the Milky Way's Carina arm

TIPS FOR STARGAZING

These tips will help you on the way to becoming an expert astronomer.

FIRST TASKS:
- ☐ Study the phases of the moon
- ☐ Track the sun's changing path over a few months

TRAIN YOUR EYES:
- ☐ Give your eyes time to adapt to the dark
- ☐ Keep them adapted—for 15 to 20 minutes (be careful, a quick look at a flashlight can undo the process!)

FINE-TUNE YOUR FLASHLIGHT:
- ☐ Tape a piece of red cellophane over a regular flashlight lens— red light hinders night vision less than white light

WATCH THE WEATHER:
- ☐ Nights when a cold front or storm has cleared out humidity and haze are best
- ☐ High-pressure zones create clear skies

TAKE NOTE:
- ☐ Track your findings in a journal!

A STAR'S LIFE

Plants and animals aren't the only things in the universe that go through life cycles—stars are born, they live, and then, when their fuel runs out, they die. How long that takes and how it happens depends on the star's size. When the fuel starts to run out, the nuclear core begins to shut down, and the star contracts. Then the temperature rises again, causing a new round of fusion in which helium atoms are forged into carbon. At this point, gravity is overcome by a new surge of energy, and the star expands. Once the available fuel is consumed, the star then sheds its outermost layers of gas, exposing the remains of the core and becoming a white dwarf—a gradually cooling ember, now stable since its energy is expelled.

ASTROFACT

BLUE STRAGGLERS ARE STARS THAT DRAIN FUEL AWAY FROM NEIGHBORING STARS TO STAY "YOUNG."

The Pleiades in the constellation Taurus

NOVAE & SUPERNOVAE

The supernova remnant Cassiopeia A in false color

Stars that suddenly becoming dazzlingly bright are called novae and supernovae. A nova's brightness varies over time—radiantly glowing for a few hours or days, and then slowly fading over the following months. Many novae go through cycles of brightening and dimming, but not supernovae. A supernova is a one-time event, the much brighter result of a dying star. While some supernovae fade quickly and die gradually, others first become red supergiants, whose stable cores grow extremely dense. When the core can no longer generate energy, the star collapses. Material from the star's outer shell rushes inward, then rebounds in a massive explosion. A supernova can release so much energy that for days or even weeks it can outshine an entire galaxy.

Hmmmm ... How can I tap into that energy?

ASTROFACT

A SUPERNOVA CAN RELEASE (BRIEFLY!) AS MUCH ENERGY AS ALL THE STARS IN THE MILKY WAY COMBINED.

EXOPLANETS

One of the great goals of astronomers is the quest for exoplanets—planets orbiting distant stars. In 1991, radio astronomers discovered the first exoplanet. Since then, technology has advanced to include superior ground-based telescopes, like Hawaii's Keck Observatory, and space-based equipment. The Hubble Telescope returned the first visual images of an exoplanet in 2008. It was named Fomalhaut b, after its parent star. The Spitzer Space Telescope has found gas-rich exoplanets with organic molecules. Since 2009, the Kepler Space Telescope has been scanning the Milky Way and has found more than 2,300 candidates for new planets.

ASTROFACT

LOCATED ABOUT 750 LIGHT-YEARS FROM EARTH IS THE MILKY WAY'S DARKEST PLANET. ITS COAL-BLACK SURFACE REFLECTS ALMOST NO LIGHT.

Artist's depiction of a Jupiter-like exoplanet and its parent star, Fomalhaut

94

PREPARE FOR LAUNCH

Fill in the blanks to complete the story about a trip into space.

Three! Two! One! Blast off! We held on to our _____
CLOTHING ITEM

as gravity forced us back in our seats. It would be the first trip

to _____, and we were _____. When out of
PLANET NAME   EMOTION

Earth's atmosphere, I turned to _____. "Did you see
NAME OF FRIEND

that _____?" Outside, it was all _____.
OBJECT   COLOR

We looked around _____. No announcement came from
ADVERB

the pilot. Finally, we fell fast asleep for _____ hours.
NUMBER

When we awoke, we had arrived at _____.
CONSTELLATION

Confused, we _____. We screamed, but there is no
PAST TENSE VERB

sound in space. That's when we spotted _____.
NAME OF ANGRY BIRD

Our hero steered us safely back to Earth! I can't wait to travel

into space again.

GALAXIES

There are an estimated 125 billion galaxies throughout the universe! And they come in three main shapes: elliptical, spiral—the largest and most massive—and irregular, which are the smallest.

Elliptical galaxies contain very little gas and dust, have almost no noticeable structure, and contain older red stars. Spiral galaxies contain all types of stars—old, young, hot and cool. Irregular galaxies are comprised of all different types of stars and large clouds of gas and dust.

The spiral galaxy M74

ASTROFACT

WHERE GALAXIES COLLIDE, BILLIONS OF STARS ARE BORN.

So many galaxies, so little time.

MILKY WAY

The Milky Way is made up of some 200 to 500 billion stars. And, it would take a jumbo jet about 120 billion years to fly across it. That's hard to believe! Our solar system is just one tiny region within the vast galaxy.

Just like objects in the solar system revolve around the sun, objects in the Milky Way orbit around a galactic center. In the middle of the Milky Way, scientists have discovered an object nearly four million times more massive than the sun: a supermassive black hole!

ASTROFACT

IF YOU LIVED NEAR THE CENTER OF THE MILKY WAY, YOU WOULD FIND THAT MILLIONS OF BRILLIANT STARS KEEP THE SKY BRIGHT ALL NIGHT.

Infrared view of the Milky Way's center

BLACK HOLES

Is a black hole really a hole? Well, a black hole's gravitational force is so strong that it can squeeze a typical star down to the size of a small town! In fact, it's so strong that nothing can escape it—not even light. This gives it the appearance of being a hole, but it's really just a superdense object.

Some people once thought that particle collisions could form a black hole on Earth. Thankfully, that is not likely. Scientists report that in the rare case a black hole did form, it would grow so slowly that we wouldn't be in any kind of danger. Whew!

SPACE DATA

THE GRAVITATIONAL FIELD AROUND A BLACK HOLE IS SO STRONG THAT IT CAN CAUSE LIGHT TO BEND.

IT IS LIKELY THAT AN EXTREMELY MASSIVE BLACK HOLE IS AT THE CENTER OF OUR GALAXY.

ACCORDING TO SCIENTIST STEPHEN HAWKING, BLACK HOLES SLOWLY EVAPORATE.

STAR LIGHT, STAR BRIGHT! CROSSWORD PUZZLE

Turn to page 157 for the answers.

ACROSS

2. Hottest stars shine this color

4. How many years can red dwarfs burn?

5. The largest stars are called _____.

7. Exploded stars

8. The size of red dwarf stars compared to other stars

9. The most common stars in the universe are called _____.

DOWN

1. Name for stars which have faded away

2. The earliest stars formed 13.5 _____ years ago

3. What is the name of of the largest star?

6. Size of the sun compared to other stars

99

LEVEL 4 ANIMALS

Let's take a walk on the wild side—through different animal habitats.

AN ARRAY OF ANIMALS

There are thousands of different species of animals across the planet. These animals can be divided into six groups, and live among five different major habits. These groups of animals include mammals, reptiles, amphibians, invertebrates, fish, and yes—even birds! Just as diverse as the types of animals are the different places they live. Animals of all kinds find home in the rain forest, desert, ocean, grassland, and even the frozen tundra.

Some animals are on the endangered species list and in peril of becoming extinct. Fortunately, Angry Birds are not!

We're tough turkeys.

Giant Pandas
(*Ailuropoda melanoleuca*)

ZOOLOGY

If you are curious about the animal kingdom, the branch of science to study is zoology. Most zoologists focus on one particular area or animal. Some even concentrate on animals that are extinct.

Let's break it down even further: zoologists study the structure, evolution, classification, and habits of animals. What does this mean? The structure is the animal's anatomy or its cells, bones, and organs. Evolution identifies where the animal came from—its origin. Classification tells us how to group and categorize the animal. Finally, studying an animal's behavior in a natural setting allows us to detect its habits.

Ring-Tailed Lemurs
(*Lemur catta*)

Elephant Seals
(*Mirounga*)

Who studies me?

FUN FACT
ETHOLOGY IS THE SCIENCE OF ANIMAL BEHAVIOR

ZOOLOGY CROSSWORD PUZZLE

DOWN

2. An animal's origin
3. To understand an animal's habits, they must be studied in this type of environment
5. A person who studies zoology is called this

ACROSS

1. Animal's anatomy
4. Some zoologists study living animals and some study animals that are _____
5. Branch of science that studies animals
6. How to group or categorize an animal
7. Animal's natural behavior is also this
8. The science of animal behavior

Turn to page 157 for the answers.

FEATHERED FRIENDS

Before we get into habitats, let's focus on one group of animals—birds! (And we don't mean just the angry ones!) You must be able to guess the most defining characteristic of all birds. Yes, feathers! They come in many shapes and colors, but they all do the same things: help with warmth, flight, and courtship. Birds are unique in that they are the only animals to have feathers.

But, many birds can do more than just fly. They can also run, jump, swim, and dive. Penguins, for instance, are not able to fly but are superb swimmers! Also, birds are as distinct as people and come in many sizes. The largest bird is the ostrich at about nine feet tall. The smallest is the two inch long bee hummingbird.

Rufous Hummingbirds (Selasphorus rufus)

WHICH ANGRY BIRD ARE YOU?

Circle the letter next the phrase that best describes you.
When finished, tally up your answers to see which Angry Bird you are most like!

1. Your friends would describe you as:
   a. Playful and mischievous
   b. Responsible and eager
   c. A practical joker
   d. Protective and judicious

2. You are this type of student:
   a. Creative, but sometimes have a hard time concentrating
   b. A keen problem solver
   c. Class clown
   d. Prefer to study by yourself

3. Your best personality trait is:
   a. Quick-minded and inventive
   b. Caring leader
   c. Unique
   d. Inner strength

4. Some might say you need to improve:
   a. Your hot temper
   b. Being a perfectionist
   c. Lacking confidence
   d. Explosive personality

YOU ANSWERED MOSTLY A'S: The Blues! You are always whizzing around with friends, quick with a joke, and making masterful creations. But, watch that temper—it can get you in trouble!

YOU ANSWERED MOSTLY B'S: Red! People know they can count on you. You are responsible and know how to solve a problem. However, don't forget: it's OK to ask for help once in a while, too!

YOU ANSWERED MOSTLY C'S: Chuck! Enthusiastic and funny, you are a unique individual that likes to make people laugh. Have more confidence in yourself—you deserve it!

YOU ANSWERED MOSTLY D'S: Bomb! It doesn't take much to set off your temper—you are the moodiest of the bunch! But, your strong morals and protective nature makes you a great friend.

NESTS

Just like us, every bird's home is unique. In fact, nests differ as much as birds do. Some construct "cups" from grass and mud; others might create a sphere of twigs; while some place sticks randomly. One thing does remain constant: the smaller the bird the more carefully created the nest.

Birds mostly build nests when they are getting ready to lay eggs. Mother birds need a place to protect their young from predators and keep them safe until they learn to fly. So, aside from raising their young, birds live almost entirely independent of their nests. If you need proof, just look at our Angry Birds!

Yellow Warbler
(*Setophaga petechia*)

Harpy Eagle
(*Harpia harpyja*)

ANGRY BIRD PINE CONE FEEDER

Make a furious feathered-friend feeder! Even Angry Birds will love this tasty treat.

WHAT YOU WILL NEED
- Ribbon
- Scissors
- Pine cone
- Knife
- Peanut butter
- Birdseed

Northern Shrike (*Lanius excubitor*)

WHAT TO DO:

1. Have an adult help you cut the ribbon.

2. Tie the ribbon around the pine cone, near the top.

3. Use the knife to spread the peanut butter all over the pine cone—don't forget to get into the grooves!

4. Sprinkle birdseed over the pine cone, so it sticks to the peanut butter.

5. Hang the bird feeder on the branch of a tree.

6. Watch the feathered friends flock to it!

BIRD-WATCHING TIPS

Similar to stargazing, beginner bird-watching requires very little gear.
Here are some tips to get you started!

- **BE A "YARD WATCHER"**
  Keep note of how many different species visit your yard over a six-month period

- **BE A "BIRD" WITH FRIENDS**
  Join a bird-watching group or simply ask friends to join you

- **LEAVE THE FIELD GUIDE AT HOME**
  Concentrate on the birds, and study their habits. Jot down just a few notes.
  Wait until you're home to look up the species. If you're too busy reading and
  writing, you might miss out on some of the bird-watching fun!

- **WEATHER WATCH**
  Try to bird-watch on drier days, or you might get caught in a rainstorm!

- **ENJOY!**

HABITATS

Let's follow the Angry Birds through five major habitats and meet some animals. But first, an introduction . . .

RAIN FORESTS

Rain forests are hot and damp, dense with trees, and absolutely teeming with animals, many of which live nowhere else on Earth.

OCEANS

Five oceans cover more than two-thirds of the Earth. To live here, animals must swim. Wait ... can the Angry Birds swim?

DESERTS

Whether hot or cold, deserts get very little precipitation. Yet they are home to more animals than you may think.

GRASSLANDS

You'll know you're in a grassland when you look around and see ... grass, of course. This habitat could be the most relaxing for the Angry Birds. Unless, you know, they run into some Bad Piggies.

POLAR TUNDRA

How could the Angry Birds keep from turning to birdcicles in places that are covered in snow and ice year-round? Do *any* animals live here? You might be surprised.

Brrr!

RAIN FOREST

The temperature is steadily high and hot in the rainforest—the perfect environment for some of the world's most beautiful and strange species!

One of these animals is the cabybara. This large rodent eats leafy greens that they find on the ground or in the water. Perhaps their strangest trait is that they are semiaquatic and like to swim! Capybaras travel in groups for protection from anacondas, like the Gaboon viper. This venomous snake uses its poison to immobilize and kill its prey and predators. Another poisonous reptile, the Golden poison frog, is easy to spot: it's a bright neon yellow color. Although the frog's color may be alluring it, don't touch it—your finger could go numb, or worse! The brightly-colored Blue Morpho butterfly has brilliant blue wings. Luckily, it is not poisonous but uses its flashy color for defense—to scare away hungry birds! Even from this small sample, you can tell the rain forest is teeming with unique creatures!

Capybara
(*Hydrochoenis hydrochaeris*)

Gaboon viper
(*Bitus gaboonica*)

114

Poison Dart Frogs
(*Dendrosatidae*)

A GROUP OF FROGS IS
CALLED A CHORUS

RAIN FOREST WORD SEARCH

Circle each word hidden below. Words will appear up, down, forward, backward, and diagonally.

LEVEL 4 ANIMALS

- ☐ CHORUS
- ☐ SNAKES
- ☐ MONKEY
- ☐ HORNBILL
- ☐ FROGS
- ☐ BUTTERFLY
- ☐ VIPER
- ☐ CAPYBARA
- ☐ RODENTS

```
D Z E O D V H O R N B I L L H
K B S T L F E L L H S V P H P
E L W H W Q K Z J E L M R R V
T T A X R I G G K W D O A O H
Z W C E B V R A D N J N B D H
Q Z P X A U N V Q L Y K V E U
S I P W A S T V Z N C E K N Y
V M S Y I T M T P S A Y Y T T
B F N K Z K P H E E P R L S J
E H G V R M M G Y R C I D Z N
C A P Y B A R A M X F S H W I
F R O G S V X D S L M L F A B
M N M J N Z X Z F J S F Y K M
D I J Y Q C H O R U S D U L A
```

Black-handed Spider Monkey (*Ateles geoffroyi*)

Turn to page 157 for the answers.

116

PAPER BUTTERFLIES

Beautiful and rare butterfly species are found in rainforests.
Makes these pretty paper decorations in vibrant colors and patterns!

WHAT YOU WILL NEED

• Tissue paper
• Pipe cleaner
• Scissors

HOW TO MAKE PAPER BUTTERFLIES

1. Pick two different colors of tissue paper. Decorate the tissue paper with patterns.

2. Cut the paper in half, then cut in half again. It should be the shape of a rectangle.

3. Pinch the tissue paper together in the middle.

4. Wrap the pipe cleaner around the tissue paper twice, right where you pinched it.

5. You will now have two ends of the pipe cleaner sticking out. These are the antenna—keep them straight or curl them around your finger.

6. Put your butterfly in a place that will make you smile when you see it!

Blue Morpho Butterfly (*Morpho peleides*)

OCEAN

Our Earth is made up of 70 percent water—and most of that is the ocean. Of course, we can't explore the ocean without discovering one of the most important underwater inhabitants: fish! Fish are so diverse that some really don't seem related at all. So, have you ever wondered: what is a fish? No matter how unique the species, all fish share two traits—they live in water and they have a backbone (in other words: they are vertebrates).

What are some of these bizarre species? The whale shark, the largest fish, gives birth to live young and eats only tiny fish, squid, and plankton. Lungfish actually gulp air! Eels have worm-like bodies and super slimy skin. And, some species, like the weedy sea dragon, are so unusual they almost don't seem real! Not all undersea creatures are fish. One thing that makes the humpback whale unique is its beautifully complex song.

Clownfish
(Amphiprioninae)

Humpback Whale
(Megaptera
novaeangliae)

Whales are actually mammals!

118

Great Hammer-
head Shark
(*Mokarran
sphyrna*)

119

DESERT

Some animals cannot survive in the hot and dry climate of the desert. But, there are many animals that thrive in this environment!

The desert tortoise is able to escape the heat by using its front legs and long claws to dig burrows in the sandy earth. These burrows are often complex—and large enough to share with other tortoises (which they often do!). On the other hand, the kangaroo rat lives a solitary, nocturnal life. They hop around on their large hind feet, which also help them kick sand over the entrance of the burrows—a good way to keep cool on a scorching hot day. The Sonora desert toad doesn't have to worry about the desert's dry air. This large toad requires little water and enjoys eating snails, beetles, spiders, mice, and even smaller toads! The thorny devil is well protected against the toad. This reptile covered in cone-shaped gold and brown scales. But, the spine's most important role is water collection and absorption—very important in the dry desert!

Black-tailed Jackrabbit
(*Lepus californius*)

Mexican Red
Knee Tarantula
(*Brachypelma smithi*)

Desert Horned
Lizard
(*Phrynosoma
platyrhinos*)

DESERT LIZARDS

NORTH AFRICAN SPINY TAILED LIZARD (*Uromastyx dispar*)
Range: Northwest Africa
Size: 15.75 to 16.93 in (40 to 43 cm)
Diet: Mainly plants, also ants and beetles

This lizard digs burrows up to ten feet (3 m) deep, where it can escape from predators and extreme temperatures. Like other herbivorous desert reptiles, it does not drink but instead obtains water from grasses and desert plants.

THORNY DEVIL (*Moloch horridus*)
Range: Great Sandy Desert in Australia
Size: 3.0 to 4.3 in (7.6 to 11.0 cm)
Diet: Ants

Thorny devils are covered in cone-shaped gold and brown scales. Their special skin gives them excellent camoflouge and protection from predators. But the spines serve another role that is especially important in the Australian desert: water collection and absorption.

VEILED CHAMELEON (*Chamaeleo calyptratus*)
Range: Border of Yemen and Saudi Arabia
Size: 10-to 24 in (25.4 to 61 cm)
Diet: Insects, some vertebrates, plants

Veiled chameleons have a very distinctive head crest, or helmet—up to two inches tall in a male. When threatened, it turns dark and curls into a ball. Like all lizards, chameleons shed their skin in patches.

MEGA MAZE

Navigate your way through this desert. Watch out for the thorny devils!

START

FINISH

Turn to page 157 for the answer.

GRASSLANDS

A grassland is a flat area of land that is covered by grasses and has few trees. Grasslands are home to an interesting and diverse collection of animals. Many of these animals are known as "browsers" (eat tree leaves) or "grazers" (eat short, fine grass). Some animals, like the pronghorn, are both! These fast creatures have a unique ability that they share with deer—they shed their prongs once a year, and then grow them again. Another grassland animal that can be found munching on leaves, flowers, and seed pods is the Masai giraffe. This subspecies is the tallest of all giraffes and can stand up to 20 feet tall! Giraffes live in Africa, as do the grand and surprisingly agile elephants! When walking, elephants place one foot in front of the other leaving behind an incredibly straight and narrow trail.

Not all grassland animals eat the shrubs and berries. The majestic lion is a predatory cat that hunts its prey. You can always spot a lion by its two distinctive features: a tufted tail and, in males, a regal mane!

Masai Giraffe (*Giraffa cameloparolalis tippelskirchi*)

Pronghorn (*Antilocapra americana*)

124

Lion
(*Panthera leo*)

125

PERSONALITY QUIZ: WHICH GRASSLAND ANIMAL ARE YOU?

Circle the letter that corresponds with the trait you most relate to.
When you're done, tally up the answers to see which grassland animal you are most like!

I. Your classmates would describe you as:
a. Natural leader
b. The strong, silent type
c. A team player
d. Very social

2. One of your best qualities is that you:
a. Stand up to your foes
b. Are an excellent secret-keeper
c. Respect your elders
d. Appreciate diversity

3. Which best describes your style? You like to wear:
a. Neutrals with a flamboyant accessory
b. Polka dots and patterns
c. One color at a time
d. Accessories, like a horn-shaped charm necklace

4. A trait that makes you unique is that you are:
a. Comfortable in large groups
b. A natural athlete
c. An excellent student
d. A vegetarian

IF YOU ANSWERED MOSTLY A'S, YOU ARE A LION!
This wild cat is a natural predator, using its majestic mane to intimidate enemies. Lions live in large groups called prides.

IF YOU ANSWERED MOSTLY B'S, YOU ARE A LEOPARD!
The beautiful leopard is a silent and secretive animal that is extremely agile as it gracefully slinks through the grass.

IF YOU ANSWERED MOSTLY C'S, YOU ARE AN ELEPHANT!
These intelligent animals work together in their herd, helping the sick or injured, and paying special care to the older ones.

IF YOU ANSWERED MOSTLY D'S, YOU ARE AN ANTELOPE!
The horned and social antelope is one of the most diverse species in the grassland, grazing throughout the day on grass, foliage, seeds, and leaves.

POLAR TUNDRA

At our planet's most northern and southern points, is the frigid and harsh polar tundra. Animals can survive the freezing temperatures by building up their fat stores to keep them warm during the long winter months. If the female polar bear is able to keep an ample amount of fat through the year, she will give birth to one or two fluffy white cubs come spring. The Arctic wolves will also give birth in the spring, often to four to six cubs. And, the pack helps with raising the cubs. When a pack member returns from a hunt, the cubs will lick the adult's mouth until he regurgitates the meat for the young wolves to eat! Wolves often hunt hares that live in the Arctic. But, it's not easy. A hare's powerful back legs help it escape its predators—hares can run up to 30 miles per hour! After an Emperor penguin lays an egg, she passes it to the father, who keeps it warm until the chick hatches—usually two months later!

Along the coast of chilly Antarctica, the slick, light gray leopard seals are also fierce predators. A large portion of their diet is krill—a small marine crustacean, similar to a shrimp—which they filter using special molars. They also like to snack on other seals, fish, penguins, and squid!

Leopard Seal
(Hydruga leptonyx)

Emperor Penguins
(Aptenodytes forsteri)

Polar Bears
(*Ursus maritimus*)

FAVORITE ANIMALS

Write down the names of your favorite animals from each habitat!

RAIN FOREST

_____ _____

_____ _____

OCEAN

_____ _____

_____ _____

DESERT

_____ _____

_____ _____

GRASSLAND

_____ _____

_____ _____

POLAR TUNDRA

_____ _____

_____ _____

Just monkeying around.

Black-handed
Spider Monkeys
(*Ateles
geoffroyi*)

LEVEL 5 SCIENCE

Science includes tons of topics, like physics, technology, and health.

A skydiver, while being influenced by gravity and the air, falls toward the Earth.

EUREKA!
YOU'VE FOUND SCIENCE

Our world is a pretty incredible place—from the physical forces of nature, to the extraordinary technology we create, and even the molecules that make up our bodies! We have successfully explored countless wonders of the natural world—and there's always more to be discovered. By studying science, we are better able to appreciate our universe.

We know how skydivers are able to change position as they free fall through the air, and what makes that opening pitch whiz through the air before the crack of the bat sends it soaring. That's the science of physics. Do you talk on a cell phone or use a computer? You can thank the science of technology for those modern miracles. Let's not forget that science even helps us save lives! Doctors study biology and medicine to do everything from fixing a broken arm to showing us the right foods to eat.

We still have yet to discover many of the mysteries of our fascinating universe, so let your imagination fly wild. You never know where science may take you—here on Earth or beyond. Let your favorite feathered friends guide you on an introduction to the wonderful world of science.

GET FLYING!

Chuck's on the right path!

PHYSICS & NATURAL FORCES

Have you ever wondered what makes a baseball soar through the air? Or an Angry Bird, for that matter? It's all physics.

Physics is about force. And interaction—the way two objects influence each other (think: an Angry Bird hitting a block!). We've all experienced force in some way or another. Pick up a heavy book. Do you feel the way it pulls you toward the ground? Or, imagine a slingshot pulling an Angry Bird. This is force. There are two common ways to measure force: the newton and the pound. A typical hardcover book weighs around 10 newtons, or 2 pounds.

Look at that kinetic energy at work!

We often credit Greek philosopher Aristotle for being the great thinker behind understanding force. But, it was really British scientist Sir Isaac Newton and Italian physicist Galileo Galilei who explored the ideas of force that we use today. They found that constant force results in constant change in motion. Kinetic energy is energy in motion. The motion doesn't change at all if there isn't any force!

FURIOUS FORCES CROSSWORD PUZZLE

ACROSS

4. Energy in motion

7. One common way to measure force

8. We use this Italian physicist's explanation of force

9. Another common way to measure force

DOWN

1. Constant force results in constant _____

2. We often credit this Greek philosopher for understanding force

3. If motion doesn't change, it is lacking this

5. We use this British scientist's study of force

6. The way two objects influence each other

Turn to page 158 for the answers.

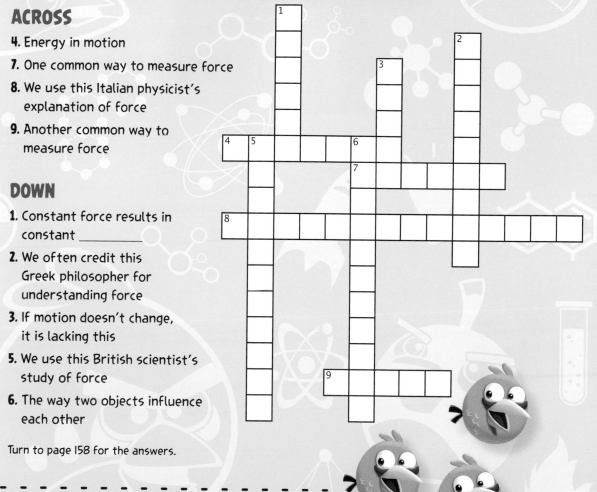

MOTION

Picture this: you've just catapulted an Angry Bird into the air. Your target? A pig. It's now soaring through the sky and is on the right path to hit the pig. Finally, it crashes into the pig's house. Success! If you've ever launched an Angry Bird, can you describe its motion? Motion is the change of position. An example of motion, in this instance, is the Angry Bird starting in position—a slingshot—flying through the sky, and ending on the pig!

To take it one step further, we can measure its displacement by determining the distance the Angry Bird travels from one time and location to another time and location: from the slingshot to the pig's house. Once we know the displacement of the Angry Bird, we can divide that by how long it took to travel this distance to determine how fast the Angry Bird is moving, which is its velocity. The velocity tells us how the position changes in time. Acceleration tells us how the velocity changes with time.

PHYSI-FACTS

WE CAN MEASURE POSITION AND DISPLACEMENT IN INCHES, FEET, OR METERS, AMONG OTHER UNITS.

VELOCITY CAN BE MEASURED IN UNITS OF MILES PER HOUR (MPH), FEET PER SECOND, OR METERS PER SECOND.

ACCELERATION CAN BE MEASURED IN MPH PER SECOND, FEET PER SECOND PER SECOND, OR METERS PER SECOND PER SECOND.

A zooming car is
another great
example of motion!

GRAVITY

Sir Isaac Newton first presented the universal law of gravitation. And it's the one force that we all experience. What happens when you launch an Angry Bird? It travels through the air until it eventually falls to the ground. In fact, it doesn't matter what you choose to launch—each and every item will eventually fall. This is the constant gravitational force at work.

A constant force means constantly changing velocity. When the Angry Bird begins to fall, it increases speed, until some other force acts on it—like a pig's house!

PHYSICS AT PLAY

START UP THE ANGRY BIRDS GAME. INSTEAD OF LAUNCHING A BIRD AT THE PIGS, TRY SOMETHING DIFFERENT. LAUNCH THE BIRD ALMOST STRAIGHT UP. THE GRAVITATIONAL FORCE PULLS DOWN ON THE BIRD, AND THIS MAKES IT SLOW DOWN.

Boo!

KERPLUNK!

Imagine you're Sir Isaac Newton.
Fill in the blanks to finish this journal entry!

As I was sitting under a _____
FOOD

tree earlier today, a _____
NOUN

fell on my head! I wondered, what

_____ force drew it toward
ADJECTIVE

the ground? After watching some other

_____ fall, I decided to call it
PLURAL NOUN

the law of _____ gravitation.
ADJECTIVE

What makes _____ fall faster
PLURAL NOUN

than _____? Gravity!
PLURAL NOUN

TERMINAL VELOCITY

Objects in free fall obtain a terminal velocity —the end of increasing speed—once the air's force pushing up matches that of gravity's pull downward. Imagine you're a skydiver. Right after jumping out of the plane, gravity's pull makes you fall faster and faster. But eventually, the force of the air beneath you matches this. Once that happens, your speed becomes constant. It's called *terminal velocity* because it's the end of increasing speed.

If you have trouble imagining this kind of air resistance, hold your hand just outside the car window next time you're going somewhere. As you go faster, the air pushes harder against your hand. Just think how hard that air would have to push against your whole body to cancel out the force of gravity!

PHYSI-FACTS

A TYPICAL SKYDIVER HAS A TERMINAL SPEED OF 54 METERS PER SECOND (120 MPH).

A SKYDIVER CAN CHANGE HER TERMINAL SPEED BY CHANGING HER BODY POSITION AND THUS THE AREA IN CONTACT WITH THE AIR.

Skydivers in free fall
can arrange themselves
in different formations.

COMPUTERS

We all use computers, but what do you know about a computer's hard drive? This important part of the computer has one job: to store programs and data until you need them. But, how is this information retrieved?

Hard drives consist of one or more rapidly spinning disks. A magnetic substance coats these disks, which are made of either glass or highly polished aluminum. Magnetic heads on a moving motorized "arm" are programmed to read and write data on the surface of the disks. IBM created the first hard drive in the 1950s, and soon all computers adapted this storage system!

TECH TRENDY WORD SEARCH

Circle each word hidden below. Words will appear up, down, forward, backward, and diagonally.

- ☐ ONES
- ☐ DOMAINS
- ☐ ZEROES
- ☐ MAGNETIC
- ☐ DIGITAL
- ☐ HARD DRIVE
- ☐ BINARY CODE
- ☐ COMPUTER
- ☐ DATA
- ☐ ELECTRONIC

```
K H C O M P U T E R V D S O X M
Z L D C G L S U F I F L I C C Z V
M U I A E O C C X D Z E R O E S S N F K
P Q G G D G W D I W X I E K M B J H O E
D V I X E A M L F V E M C L U Y E Y G L
O J T P B P D K C N K B S Q I J C O Y E
M Y A F J J O U K P T L T S U F M A C C
A V L Q F H A R D D R I V E C O W C C T
I E W M B W G T Z I G N D S J D P C P R
N J G G D N S E S H A O L C X D I X J O
S T G B T R I I E V C C I O O P K T R N
S P O D U W K L Z Y J T P B N T J P M I
R W D O V N C X R W E U R D S F M Q N C
H J M Q E U Z A A N R P T K A E S B N O
N Q G R X F N P G T E O N E S T S E N I
Q Z J N E I O A A S O F Y D F U A S P P
G B F Q B V M Z E Q G B B S R N P T K J
```

Turn to page 158 for the answers.

COMPUTER PROGRAMMING

Computer programming—or software engineering—is really just the process of figuring out a computer problem and telling the computer how to perform the solution. People who work as computer programmers do such things as analysis, figuring out how computers work, unraveling tricky situations and problems, and "speaking" to the computer in a language it understands.

This language is in the form of ones and zeroes—the binary code! The heart of computing revolves around it, and it's truly revolutionized the way we process and store digital information. Unlike the traditional system that relied on decimals, this modern method uses a base-2 system. In this way, all values can be expressed in one of two ways: ones and zeroes. Can you believe the binary code originated long before computers—as far back as the 1670s?

CRACK THE CODE

DIGITALLY, ALL VALUES CAN BE EXPRESSED IN THESE TWO WAYS:

Turn to page 158 for the answers.

HEALTH

Diet and exercise are key to maintaining good health. Through evolution, our bodies have learned to help us make decisions about which foods to eat. Thanks to the thousands of tiny taste buds on our tongues, we like to eat sugars and fats, which helped store energy to protect against the chance of famine in the old days.

Another amazing ability your body has is to design a custom-made defense system—just for you! This intricate army of germ-fighting cells is called an immune system. The immune system detects when a foreign invader enters the bloodstream. It quickly sends out antibodies to fight off the cells that make us sick.

Eating right and exercising helps us maintain a healthy immune system. That means fewer trips to the doctor's office!

Break a sweat!

Having a strong immune system means your cells have more fight in them! And that results in a healthier body and better performance—in sports and school.

MEDICINE

From its origins in ancient Greece, medicine has come a long way, and is always evolving. In the fourth century B.C., Hippocrates counseled a gentle, conservative approach to treating illness, striving to assist the body's own restorative powers. His goal, to do no harm to the patient, led to the Hippocratic oath, which is still taken by physicians today.

Today, there are new approaches taken to protect human health—from exposing people to infectious agents to stimulate immunity to fitting them with synthetic limbs so they can walk again. Cancer, heart disease, and autoimmune disorders—the "diseases of civilization"—are what doctors and researchers are fighting to cure. Scientific inquiry joins medical traditions based on care of the patient and the search for new cures.

There's no cure for Bad Piggies!

Q & A: HEALTH AND MEDICINE

1. Your body's defense system is called:

_____.

_____

2. What do sugars and fats store?

_____.

_____

3. Keep your immune system strong with

_____.

_____

4. Medicine originated with this doctor in ancient

Greece: _____.

5. Today, doctors and researchers are fighting to cure:

_____, _____,

and _____.

Turn to page 158 for the answers.

NUTRITION

We consume nutrients every time we eat or drink. Appetite is a basic instinct that helps keep us fueled, giving us the energy to get through every day. Even more important than food is water. Without water, we couldn't survive more than three days. Nutrition is extremely important. Today, public health specialists think about a third of all cancer diagnoses and an even higher proportion of heart disease is due to poor diet. Watch what you eat—but also enjoy it! Meals are a great time to gather with friends and family. Food and drink are at the center of every culture on Earth.

LEVEL 5 SCIENCE

152

ANGRY BIRDS ON A BRANCH

Make this healthy snack when
you're feeling peckish!

INGREDIENTS
- 2 Celery sticks
- Scoop peanut butter
- Handful of dried cranberries

DIRECTIONS
- Wash the celery sticks until thoroughly clean.
- Smear peanut butter into the celery stalk's groove.
- Place the dried cranberries onto the peanut butter (doesn't it kind of look like Angry Birds sitting on a branch?), and enjoy your tasty treat!

TIP: Sprinkle some shredded coconut onto your creation for a sweet surprise.

ANSWER KEY

LEVEL 1 AROUND THE WORLD

Q & A: CONTINENTS page 15

1. Africa (Nile)
2. London; Tokyo
3. Suriname
4. Lake Superior; North America
5. South

CHINESE NEW YEAR CROSSWORD PUZZLE page 19

RUNNING OF THE BULLS MAZE page 27

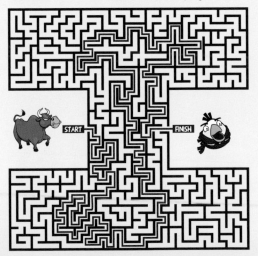

GO FOR THE GOLD! WORD SEARCH page 29

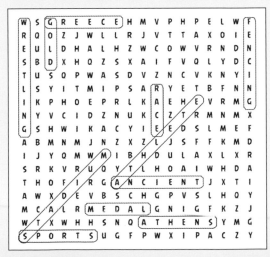

LEVEL 2 DINOSAURS

PREHISTORIC ESCAPE page 39

Q & A: EARLY CRETACEOUS page 52

1. flowers
2. Antartica
3. Magnolia, ficus, and sassafras
4. frogs and salamanders
5. snakes

CRETACEOUS PERIOD CROSSWORD page 57

Across:
2. CRATER
3. MEXICO
6. SIXTYFIVE
7. LANDMASS

Down:
1. TRIASSIC
3. MYSTERY
4. EXTINCT
5. DINOSAUR

IT'S ALL RELATIVE page 59

DINOSAURS LIVE

ON AS BIRDS

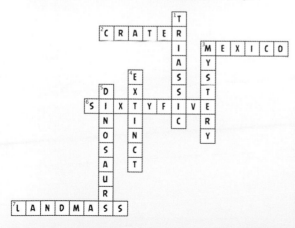

LEVEL 3 *SPACE*

OUT OF THIS WORLD WORD SEARCH page 67

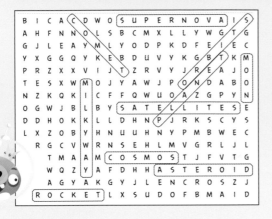

MEMORY QUESTIONS page 75

1. red
2. United States of America
3. waving
4. ocean
5. 3
6. space boots
7. reflection

MEGA MAZE page 79

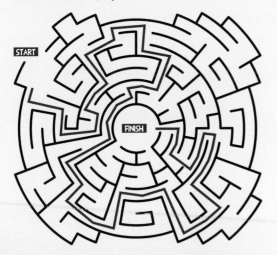

PLANETS QUIZ page 85

1. 291
2. carbon dioxide; sulfuric acid
3. liquid; solid; gas
4. Phobos; Deimos
5. 1,400
6. 8,000,000
7. 360 mph (579 km/h)
8. Triton

STARRY, STARRY NIGHT STAR MAP
page 89

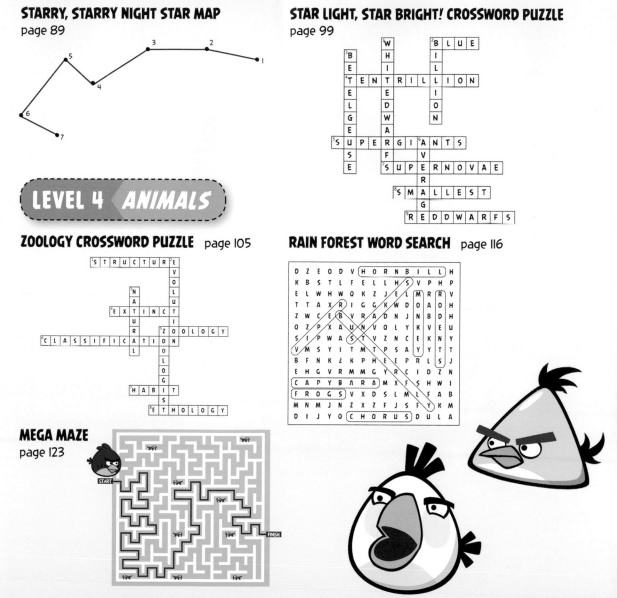

STAR LIGHT, STAR BRIGHT! CROSSWORD PUZZLE
page 99

LEVEL 4 ANIMALS

ZOOLOGY CROSSWORD PUZZLE page 105

RAIN FOREST WORD SEARCH page 116

MEGA MAZE
page 123

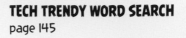

LEVEL 5 *SCIENCE*

FURIOUS FORCES CROSSWORD PUZZLE page 137

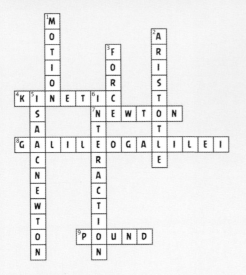

Down:
1. MOTION
2. ARISTOTTE
3. FORCE
5. ISAAC NEWTON
6. CONTRACTION

Across:
4. KINETIC
7. NEWTON
8. GALILEO GALILEI
9. POUND

TECH TRENDY WORD SEARCH
page 145

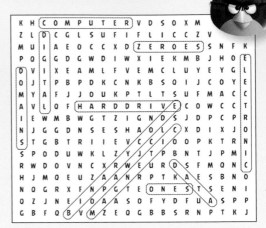

CRACK THE CODE page 147

O N E S   A N D

Z E R O E S

Q & A: HEALTH AND MEDICINE page 151

1. immune system

2. energy

3. eating right and exercising

4. Hippocrates

5. cancer; heart disease;
   autoimmune disorders

ILLUSTRATION CREDITS

Cover, wacomka/Shutterstock; Back Cover: (Studio set) iBird/Shutterstock, (Floor) photobank.ch/Shutterstock, (Images on screens) All from book interior except T-Rex by Franco Tempesta; 8-9, Bob Thomas/Getty Images; 18, ChinaFotoPress/Getty Images; 20, Jodi Cobb/National Geographic Creative; 21, Peter Molnar/Shutterstock.com; 22, Copyright © BBC Photo Library; 25, HUGHES Hervé /hemis.fr/Getty Images; 26, REUTERS/Susana Vera; 28, Ian MacNicol/Getty Images; 31, Teh Eng Koon/AFP/Getty Images; 33, Taras Vyshnya/Shutterstock; 34-38 (ALL), Franco Tempesta; 41, Friedrich Saurer/Alamy; 42-47 (ALL), Franco Tempesta; 48, Richard Bizley/Science Photo Library/Corbis; 50, Karel Gallas/Shutterstock; 51, Publiphoto/Science Source; 53-56 (ALL), Franco Tempesta; 58, Joe Tucciarone/Science Source; 60, Mark Hallett Paleoart/Science Source; 61, Raul Martin; 62-3, Vadim Sadovski/Shutterstock; 66, David Aguilar; 68-9, SOHO (ESA & NASA); 70, NASA; 71 (UP), July Flower/Shutterstock; 71 (LO), NASA/JPL; 72, photovideostock/iStockphoto; 73, NASA; 74, NASA/JPL; 77, NASA/USGS Astrogeology Science Center; 78, M. Wong and I. de Pater (University of California, Berkeley); 79, NASA, ESA, H. Hammel (Space Science Institute, Boulder, Colo.), and the Jupiter Impact Team; 80-81, NASA/JPL/Space Science Institute; 82, Science Source; 82-3, Mark Garlick/Science Source; 84, NASA; 86, John R. Foster/Science Source; 87, Miloslav Druckmüller; 88-9, Top Photo Corporation/Shutterstock; 90-91, NASA, ESA, and the Hubble Heritage; 92-3, NASA, ESA, and AURA/Caltech; 93, NASA/JPL-Caltech/STScI/CXC/SAO; 94-5, ESA, NASA, and L. Calcada (ESO for STScI); 96, NASA, ESA and the Hubble Heritage (STScI/AURA)-ESA/Hubble Collaboration; 97 (BACK), FSO/S. Gillessen et al.; 97 (INSET), Michael Hauser (STScI), the COBE/DIRBE Science Team, and NASA, 98, NASA/Dana Berry, SkyWorks Digital; 100-101, Anup Shah/NPL//Minden Pictures; 103, Lisa & Mike Husar/TeamHusar.com; 104 (UP), seewhatmitchsee/Shutterstock; 104 (LO), Jay Dickman/Corbis; 106, Bill Coster/NHPA/Photoshot; 108, Steve Byland/Shutterstock; 109, Tui de Roy/Minden Pictures; 110, Juniors Bildarchiv GmbH/Alamy; 112 (LE), Galen Rowell/Corbis; 112 (RT), Jurgen Freund/NPL/Minden Pictures; 113 (UP), Carr Clifton/Minden Pictures; 113 (CTR), Richard Du Toit/Minden Pictures; 113 (LO), Daisy Gilardini/Getty Images; 114 (UP), Pakhnyushcha/Shutterstock; 114 (LO), Ivan Kuzmin/Shutterstock; 115, Pete Oxford/NPL/Minden Pictures; 116, Konrad Wothe/FLPA/Minden Pictures; 117, Michael & Patricia Fogden/Minden Pictures; 118 (UP), Georgette Douwma/NPL/Minden Pictures; 118 (LO), Masa Ushioda/CoolWaterPhoto.com; 119, Alex Mustard/NPL/Minden Pictures; 120 (UP), Joel Sartore/National Geographic Creative; 120 (LO), Gerry Ellis/Minden Pictures; 121, Daniel Heuclin/NPL/Minden Pictures; 122 (UP), Wessam Atif/National Geographic Your Shot; 122 (CTR), Gerry Ellis/Digital Vision; 122 (LO), Matt Propert/National Geographic Creative; 124 (UP), Mike Wilkes/NPL/Minden Pictures; 124 (LO), Alan Scheer/Shutterstock; 125, Suzi Eszterhas/Minden Pictures; 127 (UP), Jo Crebbin/Shutterstock; 127 (UP CTR), davemhuntphotography/Shutterstock; 127 (LO CTR), PHOTOCREO Michal Bednarek/Shutterstock; 127 (LO), Albie Venter/Shutterstock; 128 (UP), Flip de Nooyer/Minden Pictures; 128 (LO), Frans Lanting; 129, Daniel J. Cox/NaturalExposures.com; 131, Michael & Patricia Fogden/Minden Pictures; 132-3, www.wendysmithaerial.com; 136 (Pitcher), Aspen Photo/Shutterstock.com; 136 (Ball), Alex Staroseltsev/Shutterstock.com; 139, Evren Kalinbacak/Shutterstock.com; 140 (Woman), AlenD/Shutterstock; 140 (Glass), kubais/Shutterstock; 143, Joggie Botma/Shutterstock; 144, Vladnik/Shutterstock; 146, Nils Petersen/Shutterstock; 149, isitsharp/iStockphoto; 150, Feng Yu/Shutterstock; 152, Ana Blazic Pavlovic/Shutterstock; 153, Art Wolfe/www.artwolfe.com.

Portions of the text have appeared in other National Geographic books.

ACKNOWLEDGMENTS

We would like to extend our thanks to the terrific team who worked so hard to make this project come together so quickly and so well.

Rovio Laura Nevanlinna, Jan Schulte-Tigges, Rollo de Walden, and Ilona Lindh

National Geographic Bridget A. English, Michelle Cassidy, Jonathan Halling, Karen Matthes, Meredith Wilcox, Lisa A. Walker, Katie Olsen, Judith Klein, and Marshall Kiker

Walter Foster Kathleen Spinelli, Shelley Baugh, Susan Hogan, Jessi Mitchelar, Debbie Aiken, Amanda Tannen, Jenna Winterberg, Rebecca Frazer, and Diane Cain